JANUARY SUN

One Day · Three Lives · A South African Town

RICHARD STENGEL

SIMON AND SCHUSTER

New York · London · Toronto · Sydney · Tokyo

Simon and Schuster
Simon & Schuster Building
Rockefeller Center
1230 Avenue of the Americas
New York, New York 10020

Designed by Laurie Jewell
Manufactured in the United States of America

1   3   5   7   9   10   8   6   4   2

Library of Congress Cataloging in Publication Data
Stengel, Richard.
January sun: one day, three lives, a South African town/Richard Stengel.
p.   cm.
1. Brits (South Africa)—Social life and customs.   2. Brits (South Africa)—Ethnic
relations.   3. South Africa—Social life and customs.   4. South Africa—Ethnic
relations.   I. Title.
DT2405.B75S74   1990
305.8'0096823—dc20   89-29588
CIP
ISBN 0-671-64593-5

For my mother and father

Brits (`brits), town, 25.38 S, 27.47 E; W Transvaal, S. Africa (pop. 7,688 white; 8,641 black; 1,003 Indian), founded 1924; motto: "life from water."

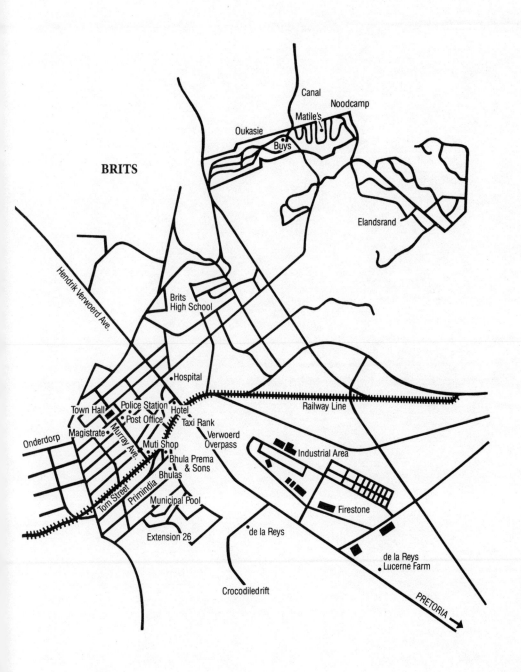

BRITS

CONTENTS

MORNING

DAWN IS DR. DE LA REY'S favorite time of day. He likes the feeling of being up and about while others are still asleep. He often chides his son Morné for being lazy and not waking at first light. At daybreak, the Transvaal sun is gentle, the only time of day when it is anything less than fierce. After eight, the rest of the day can seem like an endless afternoon. Each morning, before heading off to his laboratory, de la Rey looks out over his farm. In front of him, a field of new corn slopes down toward the Crocodile River. In the early light, the green looks somehow greener, the young plants seem to glow as if lit from within.

De la Rey's house and farm lie just off the main road to Pretoria, only a quarter of a mile from the entrance of the industrial area and the bus terminal. Yet his property feels removed, an oasis. The winding drive to his house is lined with cycads, stately trees crowned with long, spiky fronds, the direct descendants of plants that flourished 200 million years ago. The trees usher in the visitor, like tall, silent sentinels.

In Afrikaans, the cycad is known as the broodboom, bread tree in English. The plant's pith yields a starch that was used to make bread by de la Rey's ancestors, the Boers, the country's first white settlers. Yelena, his wife, is devoted to these trees, and her husband imports them specially from the northeastern Transvaal.

At the end of the drive, de la Rey has built a pond with a folly of an island in the middle, only large enough to nurture a single palm. After a rain, the pond darkens with great swirls of tadpoles and the grass teems with thousands upon thousands of tiny frogs, each no longer than a centimeter. Every step crushes hundreds of them. In Africa, de la Rey likes to say, we feel like we are still living in biblical times.

The town of Brits, where de la Rey lives, is surrounded by land that is still wild. Last year, two leopards were shot in the hills to the east. To the west, great baboons, some nearly five feet tall, patrol the ridges of the Magaliesberg Mountains. Pythons and mambas slither among the rocks. Springbok, wildebeests, and kooibok lope through empty stretches of bushveld. The town is sheltered in the lee of the Magaliesberg Mountains, less than fifty kilometers west of Pretoria and eighty kilometers north of Johannesburg.

De la Rey's house stands in an area known as Crocodiledrift, named for its proximity to the Crocodile River, where the town first began about a century ago. Brits is one of only a handful of towns in South Africa with a perennial river running through it. But the Crocodile River, despite its impressive name, is hardly awe-inspiring. In winter, it is barely more than a trickle and in summer hardly stronger than a stream. Even so, water gave life to the town, and the river allowed the first farmers to irrigate their land and grow corn and wheat and tobacco.

For the past eight years, Brits has suffered from a drought. Farmers say that droughts come in seven- or eight-year cycles. Rain is always rare in the winter, and the land becomes brown and sere. But in summer, the landscape turns a deep green. The rain comes before ten in the morning or after four in the afternoon and is never a drizzle; it pelts the skin like bullets. Summer lightning is common, and for some unknown reason, Brits is struck by lightning more than any other town in South Africa.

Christmas is high summer, the hottest time of the year. The winter months are June, July, and August. The climate is temperate, but the change of seasons is brusque. One day, it is cool and wintry, the next it is summer and broiling. Spring and autumn exist only as poetic conceits. The northern side of the Magaliesberg is frost-free and the temperature in Brits never dips below freezing.

De la Rey's land is black turf, "the best agricultural soil in the world," as he puts it. Black turf is excellent for farming because it retains water and is troublesome for building, for the same reason. It holds enough water to drown a plant or upend a foundation. Black turf is withered norite, part of the topmost layer of the Bushveld Igneous Complex, one of the world's largest and most valuable mineral complexes. Brits sits right on top of it.

The Brits district is the most densely populated rural area in South Africa, but it is still a region of dusty roads and isolated Dutch farmhouses, of tiny towns dominated by magisterial grain towers, of fields of maize stretching from one horizon to the other, of crooked sweet thorn trees laden with birds' nests.

With only coffee for fuel, de la Rey strides out his front door. He puts his head down and leans forward when he walks. He doesn't like any distraction when he has a destination, which is most of the time. His legs are considerably shorter than his son's, but when the two walk together, Morné has to skip to keep up with him.

Next to his house is a small rondavel with the distinctive thatched roof that local Afrikaners copied from African huts. On his left, he passes a run-down red barn where he stores the lucerne that he grows to feed his cattle. About two dozen cows and bulls, motionless except for their tails flicking back and forth like metronomes, stand in the muddy kraal next to the barn. Kraal is the Afrikaans word for what an American cowboy would call a corral, a term with the same Latin root, *currale*, meaning "enclosure." De la Rey's kraal, like most in the area, is a crude wooden fence made of slender trees.

Adjacent to the kraal is a simple, one-story building which functions as Dr. de la Rey's workroom, laboratory, surgery, and office. Ronald de la Rey is a veterinarian, once the only vet in town, but no longer. He used to treat all kinds of animals for all manner of illness, but does little of it anymore. Now he performs embryo transplants and artificial insemination for local cattlemen. The work is more lucrative than treatment and de la Rey enjoys the prospect of improving on nature.

A man must work to live, de la Rey often says, but he seems to live to work. He sometimes jokes that the Afrikaner is not the most industrious fellow around, but you would not know it from de la Rey. Work means freedom, he says. Work for yourself and no man can enslave you. The virtue and necessity of labor were impressed upon him at an early age by his father, who told him he had to work hard and get an education to stay ahead of the *kaffir*.

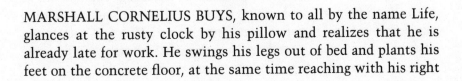

MARSHALL CORNELIUS BUYS, known to all by the name Life, glances at the rusty clock by his pillow and realizes that he is already late for work. He swings his legs out of bed and plants his feet on the concrete floor, at the same time reaching with his right hand for the pack of Rothmans on his rickety night table. He lights a cigarette and takes a deep drag, blowing out the smoke slowly, meditatively. He sits for a moment, as though unsure what to do next, then takes a swig from a brown bottle marked B & B's Kidney and Bladder Mixture ("For the relief of backache, kidney, and bladder ailments, and burning urine"). Life grimaces. He slips on the trousers he wore last night—the bottom half of a suit that he never owned—and then, barefoot and bare-chested, steps outside his dim room into the brightness of an already warm January day.

He carries a small white plastic cup filled with water, a toothbrush, and a fresh tube of Colgate toothpaste. Life prefers the taste of the American brands to the South African. They're sweeter, he says. Standing on the soft dirt outside his room, he brushes his teeth thoroughly, leaving a white smudge on his scraggly beard. He stretches his arms, glances up at the clear blue sky, and lights another Rothman.

As township houses go, Life's is spacious and solid. It has five rooms, but they are mostly empty and give the impression that someone has just moved out, rather than that anyone actually lives there. In the dining room, a small kerosene lamp sits in the center of a cracked Formica table. There is no electricity in the township.

Life walks into the courtyard. The innards of dozens of different cars litter the ground: mufflers, oil filters, fan belts, pipes, hubcaps. In front of him is the yellow carcass of an old Chevrolet, the back of which is filled with empty Castle beer cans and green bottles which once contained something called Manhattan Lemon Sting ("The international blend of tangy lemon with a lively sparkle, a 7% Perle wine, made in South Africa"). The ground around his house is a mosaic of Lion and Castle beer caps embedded in the dirt.

A short, wiry man peers under the hood of the Chevrolet. Tattooed on his back is a woman in a bikini, and on his chest, the head of a lion. He is wearing bell-bottoms and gold-colored platform shoes, the thick rubber soles of which form a wave pattern. His red baseball cap says EDDIE'S SPORTS.

Taps lives with Life's sister, in a room adjacent to Life's. Life and Taps nod at each other, but do not say anything. Taps can make even the most moribund engine turn over. He keeps all his parts in the courtyard and never throws anything out. The few cars in the township are pieced together from the parts of others; when one car dies, its organs are transplanted into another.

"I think my boss is going to fire me," Life says to Taps and smiles. Life shows no sign of haste or worry. He lives in the eternal present. For Life, the act of arriving is more important than the time he appears. And once he arrives, it's as though he's always been there. Time is where he is.

Life's large, wide-set eyes are fringed by long, feminine lashes that give him a mischievous air. This morning, like many mornings, his eyes are bloodshot and heavy-lidded.

Life goes back inside to grab an old newspaper, and trudges across the courtyard to the outhouse. Toilets in the township operate according to what is known as the bucket latrine system; in other words, everyone shits in buckets, which get picked up twice a week. Inside the outhouse, a wooden plank with a hole cut in the center rests on top of a plastic bucket. Newspapers are scattered about the floor. Toilet paper is a highly valued commodity in the township. If a roll is left around, people will routinely unravel a few sheets and stuff it in their pockets for future use.

As Life walks back to the house, two women are carrying water to their shacks from the nearby water tap, one of fifty-four in the township. The water is supplied by the white Town Council. The women wave. Tagging along behind them is a boy on his way to school, which is just on the other side of Life's house. His black-and-white woolen uniform is far too warm for weather like this.

"Hey!" Life says.

The boy turns around and trots over to him. Life puts one hand on top of the boy's head, hands him a pail, then twists the boy's head in the direction of the water tap. He scampers off. Children in the township form a ready platoon of free labor for adults. The children don't like to be collared to fetch water, buy cigarettes, or deliver messages, and sometimes try to wriggle out of it, but once nabbed, they do the chore without hesitation or complaint. One day they will be grown-ups and be able to boss around children like themselves.

The boy has to wait behind several women. Two of them have babies strapped to their backs with brightly colored cloth. One wears a battered old fedora and pushes a wheelbarrow containing a baby in swaddling blankets and a bucket of water.

Life's house occupies one of four corners formed by the intersection of two rutted dirt roads in Brits's black township. Townships are residential areas adjacent to white towns set aside for blacks. The township is known as Oukasie by its residents, an

Afrikaans nickname for Old Location, which is how the whites of
Brits refer to it. Oukasie is perched on the northern end of Brits,
where the white town's swankiest suburb rubs up against the
township.

Life doesn't want to drive today. But then, Life says, he never
really wants to drive even when he is feeling good. As he is leaving
to walk over to Buda's house, his sister Moolie hands him a mug of
tea. He tastes it and frowns. Not enough milk, my baby, he says.

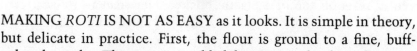

MAKING *ROTI* IS NOT AS EASY as it looks. It is simple in theory,
but delicate in practice. First, the flour is ground to a fine, buff-
colored powder. Then water is added, but it must be the right quan-
tity of water; a little more than enough is much too much. Gita
doesn't bother measuring, but always uses the correct amount.
After kneading the dough, she shapes it into balls an inch in diameter. Using a rolling pin, she stretches the dough until it is about
eight inches across. The patty is then cooked on a griddle until
slightly brown on both sides.

The Bhulas' kitchen is large and modern, the kitchen of a home
in which food has a central place. Two refrigerators flank the door,
two sinks sit under the window. A row of gleaming knives is
mounted above the stove and a series of dark skillets hangs on the
wall like musical notes along a staff.

Gita or her mother makes *roti* every morning. The bread tastes
stale after a day or two and Jai prefers it fresh. Gita's *roti* are thin
as a penny, and just as round, which is exactly the way her brother
likes them. Jai finds his mother's *roti* a bit coarse.

Gita is stacking the bread like 45s on an old-fashioned turn-
table when Jai enters the kitchen and swipes one off the top of the
stack. It is too hot to eat, and he places it next to the glass of
chocolate milk which Gita makes for him every morning. Jai removes the wax paper from the top and drinks the entire glass in
one gulp.

Jaiprakash Bhula—Jai or J.P. to everyone who knows him—is
bathed, but unshaven. Like most of the Indian shopkeepers in
town, he shaves perhaps every third day, for comfort, not courtesy.

He is tall and slender, though not so slender as his sister, whom he often chastizes for not eating enough. His hair is black and glossy, and there is just a hint of plumpness to his face.

He murmurs something to Gita. He is not awake yet. Unlike his sister and his mother, who get up at 4:30 every morning to meditate, he is not an early riser.

Today will not be such a bad day. His uncle, who is his partner in the shop, has a doctor's appointment and won't be in until after lunch. This means a little extra work, but also more freedom, a trade-off he is always willing to make. His uncle is a shopkeeper of the old school. Without his uncle, Jai will be able to read the newspapers in peace.

Jai is expecting a shipment of school uniforms. It is nearly the season when mothers troop in to buy the requisite outfits for their children. The white schools in the area generally specify somber uniforms of gray and black; the black schools sport flashier outfits with orange and blue accents. The local Indian school has no uniforms at all.

While Jai is eating, Shamu tries to climb into his lap. Jai holds the little boy away until he finishes, and then allows him to perch atop his knee. Shamu is the three-year-old son of Julia, the black servant who lives and works in the Bhula household. Shamu is cosseted by the family and is a bit spoiled. He speaks a mostly indecipherable dialect, a combination of Tswana, his mother's native language; Gujarati, the home language of the Gujarat region in northwestern India where Mrs. Bhula was born; and English. Shamu has his own miniature rolling pin—a gift from Gita—so that he can make *roti* just like Mrs. Bhula and Gita.

Jai lifts Shamu off his knee, nods to Gita, and walks out of the carved wooden front door. The house was his father's dream house and he had saved for many years in order to build it. He had plans drawn up by an Indian architect from Pretoria and used the best materials he could buy. But he only lived in the house for a few months before dying of a heart attack.

The Bhulas' house is on Carel Street, one of the four streets in the tiny grid that makes up Primindia, Brits's Indian township. To the east of the house, past an empty field, is the highway leading into town and just beyond it, the industrial area. To the west is the edge of Dr. Ronald de la Rey's farm.

Jai's battered blue Volkswagen sits in the driveway. The Volkswagen dwells outside; his father's green Mercedes resides in the garage. His father was very proud of the car, in some ways even prouder than he was of the house. The car symbolized his arrival. Nowadays many of the businessmen of Primindia have Mercedes, but not when Mr. Bhula bought his. At the moment, the car is listing slightly to the left, and Jai has been meaning to take it in and have it looked at.

Jai uses the Volkswagen to zip to and from the shop, which is less than three blocks away. Sometimes he leaves it at home for his mother to drive. She only recently passed her road test. Her husband had forbidden her to learn to drive, but she enrolled in a driving course a few months after his death.

DE LA REY REMOVES HIS GLASSES to look through a microscope at some embryo samples. With his glasses off, his face looks molelike. In the microscope's field, he sees one circle sitting on top of another, a perfect figure 8. This is a fertilized egg from a cow that he recently flushed and he is checking to see how many embryos the cow produced.

He looks up and squints to see if Richard, his cattle foreman, has everything ready. Directly in front of his laboratory is a stall where de la Rey performs embryo transfers. It is a concrete area in the center of which is an elaborate metal harness which looks like a medieval instrument of torture.

Richard uses a mop to swab the area. He wears a pair of old boots with no laces and no socks. He works slowly, methodically. When the place is clean, he scatters hay onto the floor.

Richard is an Ndebele. Most of the blacks in Brits are Tswanas. De la Rey prefers not to hire Tswanas. As a tribe, he finds them untrustworthy and unenterprising. De la Rey respects Richard and calls him "my right hand." Richard works hard, knows his own mind, and is a bit stubborn. De la Rey likes that.

"Richard has only been with me for six or seven months," says de la Rey. "He is very capable. He speaks good Afrikaans. But his assistant, Suliman, knows the cattle much better. He was my cattle foreman for years, but I fired him. He was very good with cattle. And he had an excellent memory. I would ask him how number

326 was doing, and he would reel off the information. Richard can't do that."

"But the problem was that I started paying Suliman too much money. We have a saying, pay them too much and they drink it. Suliman became a terrible alcoholic. Drinking all the time. He wasn't doing his job, so I fired him. I believe Richard has a drink now and then, but not like Suliman. Then a couple of months ago, Suliman came back and told me he had rehabilitated himself. So I thought it was right to give the man another chance. Now he's drinking less than before. But he will never be my foreman again. Even though he knows the cattle better than Richard."

De la Rey speaks directly, bluntly. The sentences emerge with declarative simplicity—subject, verb, direct object. No nonsense, no flights of fancy. Language, like forceps and syringes, is a tool.

De la Rey signals Richard to get things moving. Richard walks over to the kraal. He carries a long stick which he uses to prod the cattle. When he strikes them, he mutters *kum, kum,* in a deep, authoritative voice. He lines up three cows in the kraal leading up to the harness. Richard goads the first cow into the heavy green cage. As it nudges its head through the front, Richard clamps the bars around its neck like a guillotine.

De la Rey doffs his short-sleeved shirt and puts on a faded green, elastic-waisted jumpsuit. He is a burly man with wrists so thick he has trouble finding watchbands that fit around them. The Indian merchants in town say they have to order special extra-large watchbands for the local farmers. De la Rey's torso bears the tribal tattoo of the Brits farmer: his arms, neck, and face have been tanned a deep brown by the sun, but the rest of him, shoulders, chest, and belly, is a translucent white.

He rolls up his left sleeve and squirts some lubricant on his arm. Then he leans against the railing and plunges his left arm up to the elbow into the cow's rectum. A frown passes across his face. He twists his arm around for a few seconds, feeling for the cow's ovaries through the rectal wall. He scoops out some dung in order to clear the passageway. He is performing a preexamination to see if the cow has reacted to the hormone injection he gave it to get it to superovulate. The cow's genital organs and ovaries should be engorged.

The cow is ornery and strains its massive head against the harness. Several times, de la Rey dodges the cow's kicks. This cow is an Africander, de la Rey says, the only indigenous cattle of South

Africa. The Africander is descended from long-haired humped cattle that probably crossed into Africa from the Middle East about 2,000 B.C. The first Portuguese sailors who landed at the Cape six years before Columbus discovered America reported seeing such cattle with Khoisan tribesmen. The Africander has a large, floppy dewlap and a coffin-shaped head, but is mainly identifiable by its distinctive horns. Instead of jutting upward, the horns twist downward, giving them the appearance somehow of being upside down.

"The Africander are ranching cattle," de la Rey says. "They're not used to being in stalls. Working with them is completely different from working with European cattle, like holsteins, jerseys, and Herefords. Our farming system is different from Europe. We have big ranches, like in America. Our cattle are less calm, less docile than European cattle. The Africander likes freedom," he says with a hint of a smile. "Only American cattle are as fierce as the Africander."

These cows are donor cattle owned by local farmers. Each of the three is a show animal and is exceptionally valuable. They have been selected for their attractiveness, size, breeding ability, and bloodlines. Normally, such a cow can only have one calf a year, but with embryo transplants, the cow can produce scores. De la Rey injects the cows with hormones to get them to superovulate, that is, to produce as many as twenty eggs in a normal estrous cycle. He then fertilizes the cow with semen from a prized bull.

"We fertilize them in vivo, not in vitro," he says. In vivo fertilization occurs inside the animal and is done by hand. "We fertilize them, and seven days later we remove the eggs. The cows flushed today were fertilized seven days ago." De la Rey then implants the embryos into a carrier cow which acts as a "surrogate mother" and will give birth to a calf that is the product of two genetically superior parents.

"The quality of the carrier cows does not really matter," he says. "What is important is that they have enough milk and be a good mother. The breed does not even matter. A Guernsey can carry the embryo of a Brahman, and vice versa. The animal does not know, and nature does not care."

All three cows are ovulating and are ready to be flushed. De la Rey injects the first cow with a muscle relaxer, which prevents the cow's rectum from locking on his arm.

Richard, still as a statue, holds the animal's tail out of the way. De la Rey grips a long, steel tube, which he will insert in the animal and slide up to the cow's uterus. The tube encases a catheter. The catheter, de la Rey says, needs protection because a cow's vagina is full of dirt and the embryos must be shielded from contamination. The catheter, he explains, contains three tubes: one blocks off the uterus, one pushes a saline solution into the uterus, and one sucks out the fluid containing the embryos. De la Rey will flush both the left and right horns of the uterus.

De la Rey aims to do three cows by 9:30. On a very busy day, he will flush anywhere from five to eight, but he has done as many as fourteen cows in a morning. He prides himself on his dexterity.

"Once, we got forty-two embryos from one cow. Someone in America got eighty-four, but of course everything is bigger and better in America," says de la Rey, with a half-smile. "This is a difficult procedure," he says. "It's a technique of detail. Many small things can go wrong."

When he is finished, he gives the cow a final injection which will break down the superhormones and return it to normal. After this injection, de la Rey nods to Richard who opens up the neck brace and then pats the cow on the rump. The cow's hind legs are numb, and it reels out of the cage, wobbling and unsteady, like a drunken sailor. Richard smiles.

As Richard gets the next cow in place, Yelena tells her husband that a farmer has just phoned to ask whether his cow was pregnant yet. De la Rey looks at her quizzically and says that it is far too early to know. Then he smiles and says that he suspects the farmer knows it's too early, but that the old boy was just looking for an excuse to have a drink.

LIFE STROLLS UP TOKA STREET toward Buda's house. Toka Street is the one road in the township with a name. Dr. Toka, as he was known, was Oukasie's first town councillor in the 1940s and something of a dandy. He was neither a medical doctor nor a Ph.D., but because he had studied briefly in England, everyone called him doctor as a sign of respect.

Toka Street, like every other thoroughfare in the township, is an uneven dirt road. But Toka Street is Oukasie's Broadway, the township's main artery, and winds its way from the bottom of Oukasie to the top.

Oukasie itself is long and skinny; 2.2 kilometers in length and no more than 300 meters wide. The land was originally part of Johan Brits's farm and was set aside for black habitation by the local government. From above, Oukasie looks like a messy gash in the earth. On its long northern boundary rises a koppie (the small, craggy hillocks common to the area), while to the south is the white residential area. The population of Oukasie was about 15,000 in 1985, but now it is probably less than half that. Oukasie has fifteen churches, one nursery school, one high school, and six shops.

The walk to Buda's house takes only a minute or two. Buda owns the township's largest taxi service—six cars. The taxis, known as kombis, are actually small vans that can seat about eight comfortably, but usually carry twelve or thirteen.

Everyone in Oukasie greets each other when they pass.

"Hello, Ma!" Life calls out to a middle-aged woman.

"Hello, Life!" she sings back.

A young fellow walks by. "Allo, allo," Life says quickly.

"Dumela. Dumela," ("Good morning" in Tswana) Life says to two men passing by.

Two older women approach on their way to the water tap.

"Hello, Ma. Hello, Ma," Life says.

"Lagi?" one replies. (Tswana for "How are you?")

"Lagi? Ma!" Life says.

"Akee! Akee!" they call back, which means "fine."

Two young women approach. Life gives them a raised eyebrow and a soft dumela. One girl averts her eyes but her friend calls out, "Hello, Life!" The two giggle. Life nods his head and smiles. It might not be such a bad day after all.

"We must say hello to everyone we see," Life says. "Everyone who walks by. That is what we are taught. It is not like the white man. The Boer," he says, "is humorless. I've never seen him laugh."

In Oukasie, the men are small and narrow and the women are small and wide. The men look older than they are and the women, younger.

Life passes only one person who does not acknowledge him: a young man with a cassette player on his shoulder blasting American disco music. Life shakes his head in a gesture of, *these-kids-today*. Life, like many in Oukasie, is concerned about "the youth," as young people in the township are invariably called. "It's the same all around the country," he says. "The youth are a problem. They have nothing to keep them busy."

This stretch of Toka street is dotted with stucco houses built in the 1930s when Oukasie was first "established" by the white authorities. Some have verandas, rusticated columns, and tile roofs. But there is none of the nostalgia of age about them; they're just falling apart. In Oukasie, even the dirt seems worn.

Most of the houses in Oukasie are metal shacks: four zinc walls topped by a flat roof of corrugated iron. The shanties are often quite fanciful. People use the flat roof as a storage area, an attic without walls. The tops are piled high with loops of barbed wire and planks of wood, bricks, tires, parts of bicycles and baby carriages, shoes and suitcases—anything that someone does not want to throw away, which is everything. The objects serve another purpose: holding the roof down. Others use large stones instead, strategically placed like rooftop paperweights.

Some shanties combine the shabby and the sumptuous. Life passes one that sprouts a large and complicated television aerial. Many houses have some touch of decoration: a cactus plant by the door, a rock garden, some pieces of tile arranged in a pattern. Clotheslines are strung across front yards. Hung with bright fabrics, reds, yellows, cobalt blues, they provide a touch of gaiety, like fluttering penants on a broken-down cruise ship.

Coal is used for heat and cooking. Mounds of it, like drifts of black snow, are stored in the front yards. At dusk, the air of Oukasie is smudged; a cloud of smoke hovers a few feet above the township. The residents of Brits's new white housing development, Elandsrand, which abuts Oukasie, regularly complain that the smoke ruins their view and poisons their air.

Most shanties, no matter how humble, boast some kind of fence. The fences are often made of bits of barbed wire or mattress coils, their curlicues strung together to form a whimsical wire border. The partition is not to keep anyone out; it is more a line of demarcation, a way of saying, *this is mine.*

Some of the older houses look as if they have been hit by aerial bombs. Roofs ripped off, bricks strewn about, shards of glass scattered everywhere. These are the houses of the people who have

moved to Lethlabile, the new "model township" which the government has built twenty-four kilometers to the north at a cost of 32
million rand.* The government wants everyone from Oukasie to
move there. Those who did so were handsomely compensated for
their houses, which were then promptly demolished by the authorities so that no one else could occupy them. In 1986, as part of this
policy, Oukasie was officially "deproclaimed" or "disestablished,"
as it is sometimes known. Technically, the township no longer
exists. According to law, it is now a nameless squatters' camp.

Buda's shanty has had so many additions it is hard to pinpoint the
nucleus of the house. Buda was a poor man, but as he began making
money he started adding rooms. In the dirt front yard of the house,
in the shade of a jacaranda tree, a few men are sitting drinking beer.
Goats meander through the yard. A large emaciated dog sniffs
around for scraps. Naked sniveling children wobble for a few steps
before falling in the dirt.

The taxi business is the one growth industry in the township.
All day long, a few dozen taxis rumble through Oukasie taking
people to and from town, to shop or work. A trip from Oukasie into
town costs sixty cents. A public bus—Bophuthatswana Transport
—leaves from the entrance of Oukasie and goes to the Thari terminal in town, but it is inconvenient. People prefer taxis. The taxi
service is essentially a large family car-pool. Sometimes, Life seems
to be merely chauffeuring his friends around town.

"You're late, man," Buda says. Life smiles and lights a cigarette. His expression says, I know and you know that it doesn't
really matter.

Buda is a skinny, nervous man. He is an Ndebele, one of only
a handful in Oukasie. Besides Ndebeles, there are a few Xhosa,
Sotho, and Shangaans, but Tswanas predominate. Buda's father
came down from the north and found work on a farm. The Ndebeles are reputed to be shrewd businessmen and Buda seems to
validate the stereotype. He bought his first taxi in 1981 with a
R8,000 loan from his father. Then he started buying old kombis
and fixing them up. He made money from the first day.

Buda is the butt of many jokes. The drivers say he is always

---

* Money is expressed in rands throughout the book. At the time, one rand
equalled about two dollars. To get the dollar amount, divide the number of
rands in half.

after their women. He tells the drivers that if they let him sleep with their wives or girlfriends, he will pay them double. The drivers laugh at him and pretend that they are arranging it.

Life picks up a yellow atchaar bucket filled with water. Atchaar, an extremely spicy condiment made from green mangoes, is a staple of township diet not only because of its piquancy but because the plastic containers it comes in make ideal water carriers.

Life grabs a rag, and begins to clean the dusty white kombi sitting in front of Buda's house. He makes halfhearted swipes at the handles, the seats, the steering wheel. The rag looks at least as dirty as the surfaces he is wiping off.

Stubbing out his cigarette, he climbs into the driver's seat. Buda has given him a burlap bag of money for the day. Life counts it twice—R45.20. He doesn't want Buda to be able to accuse him of filching any. Drivers make about R100 for a full week's work. Life seldom drives for a week straight. Only when he has bills to pay. Usually he fills in for a day or two.

The keys to the taxi are at one end of a twelve-inch purple-colored rabbit's foot. All the taxi drivers use them. Some are longer, some shorter, but all are colorful and furry. "So the keys don't get lost," Life says.

The kombi starts on the second attempt, and Life pushes the hand gear into first and rumbles off. The car rattles as it makes its way down the rutted road. The front of the kombi bobs up and down like a boat going over rough waves. It has no shock absorbers. The road is an obstacle course of rocks, holes, and bumps, as well as skittering dogs and children. Life steers clear of the rocks and holes; the dogs and children can take care of themselves.

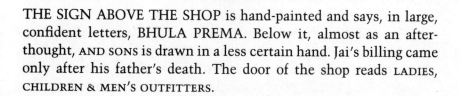

THE SIGN ABOVE THE SHOP is hand-painted and says, in large, confident letters, BHULA PREMA. Below it, almost as an afterthought, AND SONS is drawn in a less certain hand. Jai's billing came only after his father's death. The door of the shop reads LADIES, CHILDREN & MEN'S OUTFITTERS.

The shop is part of an arcade of 1930s buildings with sloping tin-roofs and slim Doric columns that make up the shopping area of Primindia. Bhula Prema and Sons is on Kruis Street, just off Tom Street, Primindia's principal shopping avenue. Shopkeepers in Primindia open for business at eight, at least half an hour before stores in the white business area. Like the other shops on Kruis Street, Bhula Prema and Sons looks as though it could be a general store in a frontier town—which, in fact, it once was.

Kruis Street is a spit of a road that crosses the railway line that separates the white area from the Indian. Everything north of the tracks is white. In 1955, Primindia became the first proclaimed Indian township under the Group Areas Act, which demarcated all land in South Africa according to racial classifications. The act updated the Native Land Act of 1913 and the Development Trust and Land Act of 1936, the cornerstones of residential segregation and group "identity" in South Africa. Under the Group Areas Act, residential areas in South Africa were designated according to the government's four standard racial classifications: white, black, Coloured (which refers to those of "mixed race"), and Indian or Asian. In Brits, the railway line had already marked a de facto separation between white and Indian, but the ruling hardened custom into law.

At this hour of the morning, the street is still sleepy. Even the dust, which by late morning blankets the cars and shop fronts, is yet to be roused. Jai swings the Volkswagen into a parking place in front of the shop and rummages in his pocket for coins. Twelve minutes for five cents; thirty for twenty. The meters in front of Checkers, Jai says, the grocery store in the white business area, provide thirty minutes for five cents, an hour for twenty.

He unlocks the padlock on the metal gate and then quickly opens the two ancient locks on the front door. Every morning he is met by the same musty air. The shop is choked with merchandise. Every inch of space is used to store or display something for sale. Wooden shelves stretch from floor to ceiling, loaded down with shirts. Dozens of ladies' shoes, in a rainbow of colors, are fastened with pins to the edges of the shelves.

A horseshoe-shaped arrangement of old wooden glass cases looks like a museum exhibit of unwanted goods from the 1950s. Clunky rotary watches from Eastern Europe, shiny rings with imitation jewels, cheap plastic sunglasses, ballpoint pens, bow ties, knives, and one large harmonica. The store has a whitewashed, molded tin ceiling and an ancient fan in the center that revolves so slowly it seems hardly to stir the stale air.

Jai would like to spruce up the place. Make it more contemporary and fashionable. He thinks local blacks are becoming more sophisticated about clothes, and he wants to cater to them. His uncle is not so sure. His uncle views change of any kind with misgiving; he is a man who does things the way they have been done before.

Jai walks to the rear of the shop and reaches underneath the cash register for an old shoebox. He takes out the morning's "float" —money left over from the night before which will be used to begin the day. Jai puts one hundred rand—the bills are all soft and worn —in the register. The machine, unlike virtually everything else in the shop, is high tech: a sleek Olivetti that hums in contrast to the clatter of the matronly Victorian register sitting on the far counter. The old cash register, with its stiff keys marked "Pounds" and "Shillings," was purchased by Jai's father when he started the shop. Now it is used to store buttons. The counter next to the register was where Mr. Bhula once measured out sugar and coffee to sell to farmers.

Moments later, the first of the shop's two workers arrives. Mabel is a sturdy woman of about twenty, with a sly manner that suggests she knows a great deal more than she lets on. Mabel lives in Bethanie, just over the border in Bophuthatswana, the black homeland which was given "independence" in 1977. Homeland is the term used by the government for what was once known as "reserves" and "Bantustans," supposedly sovereign countries which were created to accommodate all black South Africans and remove them from white urban areas. Without saying hello, Mabel slips a blue-and-white smock over her dress, takes a broom from behind the door, and begins to sweep.

While she works, Henry arrives. A stooped, grizzled black man, Henry has worked at Bhula Prema and Sons for fifteen years and is as much a fixture as the old cash register—and about as useful. Henry arrives every day by bus from Maboloka in Bophuthatswana. He avoids looking anyone directly in the eye. Henry calls Jai *baas*, no matter how many times Jai tells him not to.

Neither Mabel nor Henry is a member of a union, but Jai's uncle fears that one day they will join. Mabel was recently approached by some union organizers from the industrial area. Jai's uncle says he will fire her if she becomes a member. Jai believes unionization is inevitable. "The Indian merchants," he says, "don't understand the unions. They feel like the unions are trying to take over their business. They ask their workers, why are you joining the union? Haven't we always treated you well? They regard themselves as benevolent employers."

Jai takes some change from the till and hands it to Henry. Henry returns five minutes later with copies of *Business Day* and the *Johannesburg Star.* Jai looks forward to his newspapers; they are the highlight of his morning. He doesn't read any Afrikaans papers. Sometimes, if things are particularly quiet, he will read *Business Day* twice.

Two young black women enter the store. They step in gingerly as though they are unsure of how they will be received. Blacks in Brits often walk in the front door as though they would be more comfortable entering through the back door. The women are from Oukasie. They talk to Mabel in quiet tones. Mabel informs Jai that the women are looking for a child's skirt.

"How old is she?" Jai asks. Mabel confers with them in Tswana.

"Two years," she says.

Jai does not speak Tswana, the first language of most of his customers. He knows a few phrases, which he sometimes drops into conversation. Mabel is the resident interpreter.

Mabel takes out two types of skirt. They are tiny things. One has a pink, plastic stripe down the side; the other is unadorned.

"It's up to you," says Mabel, who routinely mixes English and Tswana. "Both are nice."

The two women whisper to each other, and then the shorter of the two shakes her head no. She wants to see something else. They look around, and the taller points to a khaki-colored jumpsuit with red trim. It's cheaper than either of the two skirts. They both smile; they'll take this one.

"Some shoes, perhaps?" Jai says from behind the counter.

"What is the price?" asks the shorter one.

"Well, we have different styles," says Jai, who then makes a sweeping, theatrical gesture that takes in all the shoes hanging on the wall. They nod. As with most of Jai's customers, style is a secondary consideration to price. Customers want to know the price first, then they decide whether they like the shoe. Jai has been ordering more fashionable shoes in a variety of styles and colors. His taste and his customer's pocketbook do not always correspond.

"The factory workers who come into the shop are more sophisticated than the farm workers," he says. "The factory workers who live in town know they want a particular style, and if you don't have it, they walk out. The farm worker comes in and says he wants a pair of shoes for twenty rand."

An old domestic enters. Beige beret, blue smock.

"How are you, Mama?" Jai says.

She wants a pair of white shoes. Jai spins around and plucks a pair from the wall.

"Here you are, Mama," Jai says. She likes them. How much?

"R89.99, Mama," Jai says. She seems to be weighing this.

"Not more, not less," she says evenly, raising her eyebrows.

"Sorry, Mama. R89.99," Jai says. She has come to a decision. She nods okay. Using a pocket calculator, Jai adds on the 12 percent sales tax.

"R100.79," he tells her.

"No, no," she says, shaking her head firmly, as though she has been tricked.

"Sales tax, Mama," Jai says evenly.

"But I don't have it," she replies. Reaching into her brassiere, she takes out five dog-eared R20 notes and lays them slowly on the counter. They are as soft as crepe de chine.

"That's all," she says, looking rather forlorn. Jai considers this.

"No problem, Mama," he says. He takes the money and she takes the shoes and walks out of the shop happy, calling airily behind her, "Thank you."

Jai's father would have scoffed at him for using a calculator. Mr. Bhula could do such calculations faster in his head. His ability was not unique; virtually every Hindu merchant of his generation could multiply complicated fractions and three-figure numbers without pencil and paper. As boys, they had all been forced to memorize complicated multiplication tables at Gujarati school. Years of shopkeeping streamlined the mental arithmetic. Jai's generation depends on the microchip.

"I can remember my father reading figures with two fingers," Jai says. "He would run them down the line of numbers. He was faster than any calculator. He didn't trust the calculator because you had to type the numbers into it, and you might get them wrong. Besides, having to type in the numbers slowed him down."

●

A MASSIVE BRAHMAN BULL shifts and clatters in the green metal harness. Richard uses a soapy rag to wash the pink tongue of the bull's penis. Then he crouches down and snips tufts of hair from the sheath. When he's finished, he places a leather cross-stool in front of the bull for de la Rey.

De la Rey sits down heavily. Richard has fetched a large metal device, roughly the size and shape of an M16 rifle. He plugs the ejaculator into a nearby outlet. It is then placed on the bull's penis, shooting electric currents into the shaft which cause the bull to ejaculate. The ejaculator is an American product which de la Rey says is proscribed under Congress's 1986 limited sanctions law. No company in South Africa makes them and they are absolutely essential to de la Rey's work. If you need a product from America, he says, there are always ways around the restrictions.

This particular bull is owned by a local farmer and is of American patrimony. It was born in Texas, raised in Brazil, and shipped to South Africa through a third country in order to evade any potential restrictions. The farmer doesn't advertise the birthright of his bull.

Brahmans look like creatures designed by a quarrelsome committee. They have ears that droop halfway to the ground, thick folds of skin around the neck that swag even farther down, and an enormous rubbery hump that rises from its back.

The Brahman, de la Rey says, *should* be the indigenous bull of South Africa. The animals came originally from India, but they adapted perfectly to the South African climate. Heat doesn't bother them. They need little water and almost no maintenance.

"The hump is fatty connective tissue," de la Rey explains. "It evolved from their need to survive in the desert, and it enables them to go for long periods without drinking or eating. They are tough and stubborn." The Afrikaner sees himself in the Brahman: a rugged, imported breed that adapted perfectly to Africa.

. . .

Richard presses the ON button. An electric current jolts the bull. Once. Twice. Three times. Richard pauses for fifteen seconds between each shock. The ejaculator has a built-in computer which automatically increases and decreases the impulse. The bull is twitching and begins to shudder.

De la Rey holds a plastic funnel underneath the bull's penis. On the bottom of the funnel is a rubber tube shaped like an inverted dunce's cap. As the bull begins to ejaculate, de la Rey catches the semen in the funnel. It slides down into the rubber cone and then the test tube. The semen is yellowish, viscous, and has a sharp smell.

"It's beautiful, eh?" de la Rey says and smiles.

De la Rey takes a test tube of semen into his workroom. With an eyedropper, he places a drop of it on a slide. Often he makes a rough semen count like this immediately after the procedure.

"It's only magnified ten times," he says, "but you can see the wave movement. This is very good semen." The view under the microscope reveals a landscape of thousands of tiny black sticks twitching wildly against an orange background.

Small amounts of semen are deposited in clear plastic straws only a millimeter or two in diameter. The straws are marked and then placed in liquid nitrogen chilled to 192 degrees below zero. Frozen semen, says de la Rey, can be kept alive indefinitely. Even after the semen is diluted, each straw will contain well over a million sperm. In theory, with artificial insemination and frozen semen, a bull can father thousands of calves a year.

"There are two basic groups of cattle," de la Rey says. "You get what they call *Bos taurus* and *Bos indicus*. The *Bos taurus* are mainly a European type of cattle, like the Simmental, the Hereford, and the Angus. *Bos indicus* are humped cattle like the Brahman, the Africander, the Bontmara. If you're crossbreeding between these two main groups, you don't get what we call hybrid vigor."

De la Rey is a cattle eugenicist. Embryo transplants are a way of improving the species by combining the best characteristics of different parents. De la Rey does not hesitate to extrapolate from the animal kingdom to the human. "If you cross a Simmental and a Brahman, you're taking two good qualities and mixing them. If you cross a black and a white, you're crossing bad and good. If you cross the Simmental and the Brahman, you get improvement. You don't get improvement with black and white. It's a bad hybrid. When you see that a cross is bad, you don't carry on doing it."

De la Rey feels no compunction about making generalizations about race. Anthropologists, he says, make statements about racial characteristics all the time. As a veterinarian, he must generalize about different species of cattle: Guernseys are gentle, Africanders are obstinate.

Every day, he says, people make observations about ethnic or national differences: Italians are warm, the English are cold. Only when people generalize about blacks is it considered unfair and bigoted. Why shouldn't he point out differences between black and white, or between one black tribe and another? The Tswanas, he suggests, are weak and devious. The Zulus, by contrast, are proud and aggressive. "You'll never find a Tswana working in a mine like a Zulu," he says. "The Tswanas would rather be clerks."

All human analogies are imperfect, he notes, but there are certain things that one can assert with confidence. The blacks are the way they are, he suggests, as a result of nature *and* nurture. Their environment plus their genetic inheritance combined to keep them down.

"I think a person must not be too strict on the distinctions between the environment and genetic inheritance," he says. "The one very often leads to the other." Environmental factors, if continued over time, ultimately become genetic ones. A cow, he says, which is not well fed or well treated will produce a less genetically fit animal than the same cow would if it were looked after properly. If this is repeated over and over again, the species will degenerate. "Different species," de la Rey says, "adapt in different ways."

African culture, he says, has always been based on survival of the fittest. In Africa, the least fit to survive were always pushed southward, eventually arriving in the vicinity of South Africa. "The tribes came down from the north," he says, "and fled from the other stronger tribes. All the smaller and weaker tribes of Africa drifted down to South Africa."

The most powerful tribe in South Africa, de la Rey says, is the white Afrikaner. This belief is universal among Afrikaners, who suggest that blacks must not be treated as a monolithic group, but a cluster of ten different and often hostile nations. Whites make up roughly 16 percent of the population of South Africa, about 4.8 million, and English-speaking whites, descendants of British immigrants, constitute a little over a third of that number. Only the

6 million Zulu, de la Rey says, the largest black tribe among the country's 24 million blacks, can rival the Afrikaner. De la Rey smiles and says he is a member of the white tribe of Africa.

"And perhaps we are an endangered species, eh?" he says.

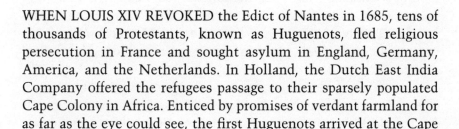

WHEN LOUIS XIV REVOKED the Edict of Nantes in 1685, tens of thousands of Protestants, known as Huguenots, fled religious persecution in France and sought asylum in England, Germany, America, and the Netherlands. In Holland, the Dutch East India Company offered the refugees passage to their sparsely populated Cape Colony in Africa. Enticed by promises of verdant farmland for as far as the eye could see, the first Huguenots arrived at the Cape of Good Hope in 1689.

By the time Pieter de la Rey arrived at the Cape about a century later, the French language had almost disappeared and his fellow Huguenots had intermarried with the local Dutch burghers. Pieter de la Rey followed suit, marrying Hester Nel and fathering ten children.

By the late eighteenth century, the Cape community had formed its own distinctive identity. The people were known as Boers—farmers—and they called themselves Afrikanders, later Afrikaners, the people of Africa.

The de la Reys farmed with the help of the local black tribesmen at the Cape and learned the language of the Boers, Afrikaans, a simplified Dutch with a medley of new words of African coinage. Little changed when the territory first came under British rule in 1814. But the British attempted to Anglicize the Boers, and in 1834, when Britain ordered the emancipation of slaves in every region of the empire, the Boers bridled at the interference in their affairs. They would treat the natives as they saw fit. The Protestant zeal which had brought them to a new land did not extend to the continent's pagan souls.

The following year, the de la Rey clan set out on the Great Trek, an exodus of six thousand farmers and their families who loaded their ox wagons and their muskets and struck north across the Orange and Vaal rivers beyond the northeast frontiers of the colony. They trekked through a dry, inhospitable land where trees offered little shade and the sky even less rain.

"The Voortrekkers believed that God was providing for them," says de la Rey. "They didn't quite think they were the Chosen People. They believed that if they abided by His wishes He would provide for them. It's the belief of the Afrikaner that God is fair. If you hold up your side, He will uphold His."

By 1837, the Voortrekkers were headed toward the western Transvaal and realized they would have to pass through the kingdom of Mzilikazi. Mzilikazi, the former lieutenant to Shaka, king of the Zulu, led a fierce tribe in the Magaliesberg region of the western Transvaal. They were known as the Matabele: *Ma*, meaning people, and *tebele*, referring to the tall, ox-hide shields they carried into battle.

In one of the bloodiest encounters between Boer and black man in the nineteenth century, the Matabele's assegais proved no match for Boer rifles as an expedition force of Voortrekkers, including Adrianus de la Rey, repelled an army of thousands of warriors. Hundreds of Matabele were slain; the Boers did not lose a single man.

Part of the de la Rey clan settled in the Northwest Free State and part in the western Transvaal. At the end of the nineteenth century, the Transvaal was made up of small, self-reliant, trekker communities. They were a terse, rugged people whose lives were shaped by the strictures of an Old Testament God and the demands of an equally unforgiving landscape. For the Boers, the Enlightenment of Europe had never pierced their darkness. Their intellectual curiosity had diminished as their distance from civilization had increased.

The farmers' houses had three or four small rooms. The floors were made of clay and were given a hard, smooth finish with dried cow-dung. They built sturdy furniture out of fragrant tambouti and yellowwood. The farmers grew wheat and corn, as well as peaches, oranges, sweet potatoes, cabbage, and pumpkin. But farming in the Transvaal was not the *lekker lewe*—the sweet life—that it had been on the Cape. In summer, insects and tropical disease killed off many cattle, while hailstorms devastated young plants.

In 1899, when war again broke out against the British, the local farmers did not think twice about taking up arms against the despised colonial power. "Most of the men in my family became leaders in the Anglo-Boer War," de la Rey notes. "They were a very confident, very disciplined, militaristic people. There were six brothers in each family and they were leaders in the war." One of those farmers was Koos de la Rey, an austere Boer general and a formidable advocate of Afrikaner nationalism. De la Rey rode a fleet Basuto pony and carried into battle only a pocket Bible and a sjambok, a heavy, leather whip favored by the Afrikaner.

As commandant of the western Transvaal, General de la Rey was one of the first practitioners of guerilla warfare, a technique that confounded the tradition-bound British. De la Rey would order his troops to retreat and draw British columns after him; then he would swing around and assault the enemy's flank. At the Battle of Silkaatsnek, just outside of Brits, de la Rey led one of the Boers' most heralded victories, a bold ambush on the British forces under Lord Roberts.

For nearly a year, the commandos in the Transvaal held the British in check, but eventually the Boers were worn down. Lord Kitchener, the High Commissioner of the Transvaal, was merciless. British soldiers were ordered to raze hundreds of farms in the Brits area. Kitchener then set up concentration camps for the displaced Boer civilians. During the war, some 26,000 people perished in these camps, 20,000 of them under the age of sixteen. "My grandmother was the only one of her sisters to come out of the camps alive," says de la Rey.

The Boers surrendered in 1902. Kitchener's slash-and-burn strategy had a devastating impact. For years afterward, destitute Boer families in the Transvaal could be found by the side of the road selling fruit and trinkets.

De la Rey's father was born on a farm in the western Transvaal. His family was poor, and he went to work early, never getting past the sixth grade. He had been left a small plot, but he found that he could not support his family by farming. He took a job with the South African prison service and within a few years he became warden of a prison in northern Natal. His second son, Ronald de la Rey, was born in Zululand and was raised in prison service housing.

"We were exposed to the prison and sheltered from it at the same time," de la Rey recalls. "When we were small, we lived a long way from the prison and we never heard anything about it. We used prison labor in our garden. You could get them very cheap. We saw them and knew them, but we kept apart. Gradually we were let in on what was going on. It was actually a jail built for the farmers' purposes so the criminals could work on the farms.

"I was in secondary school near Leslie. There, we lived close to the jail. We heard and saw more. Most of the blacks put in these country jails were there for tribal murders. At Leslie, eighty percent of the prisoners were Zulus. Some of them had killed Indians in Natal, near Durban. They were a good people. They had killed Indians, but they did it out of a tribal feeling, a sense of group freedom, like a war.

"It worried me a bit that they were in prison, but when you're a young boy and you work with these people, you never had the feeling that they were going to assault you. We didn't stand behind them with a gun. They weren't a common type of criminal. They had done what they had done for other reasons."

De la Rey respected the Zulus. "We knew them. We spoke quite a lot of Zulu in our house. We sometimes used it among ourselves. When my father wanted me to do something with the blacks, he would instruct me in Zulu, so they would know as well. My mother was very good in Zulu. She was brought up in northern Natal and spoke Zulu with her brothers and sisters."

As a boy, the strict Calvinism of the Dutch Reformed Church suffused his daily life. "You got up, you read the Bible, and you prayed. There were prayers in the morning, at lunch, and before and after dinner. We lived what we believed in. We didn't take things for granted. We grew up with the idea that being a Christian is not just for Sunday, but for everyday living."

The year de la Rey entered the University of Pretoria, his father accepted a job as warden of Brits Prison. Brits Prison was less a jail than a work farm; the inmates were blacks who had committed misdemeanors like disturbing the peace. The farm grew cabbages and onions and the prisoners worked in the fields.

At Pretoria, de la Rey studied veterinary science and qualified in 1962. "We grew up with a fanatic desire to study, to be better than both the English and the blacks, to be in command. You know, after the war, the Afrikaner was very poor. My father always said to me, if you don't get educated, the kaffir will be your boss. My eldest brother is a teacher with a double degree. My other brother is an accountant with a law degree. Of our grandparents, the only one with a matric [a high-school degree] is my wife's mother. My mother is grade six. They were ill-educated because of circumstances, not because of intelligence. There was an obsession with learning."

De la Rey became absorbed by politics at the university. "I always had a major interest in politics," de la Rey says, "even as a boy. I remember in 1948 when the Nationalists took over from the United party. My parents were Nationalists, the party of apartheid. I had been in the Nationalist party from the moment I opened my eyes."

"But I broke from the Nationalists in Verwoerd's time when I was at university and he came to give a speech. At the time, I was on the Student Council. I was voted in by the students. The University of Pretoria was the biggest university in the country. At that stage, they had forty to fifty thousand students. I didn't campaign. I don't campaign."

Prime Minister Hendrik Verwoerd was the intellectual architect of grand apartheid and the theorist behind the policy of "separate development," the idea of a white South Africa surrounded by independent black areas. "The idea in 1962 was like this," says de la Rey. "Verwoerd and the Nationalists said every black is a citizen of a homeland, and South Africa is the white land."

"After Verwoerd finished speaking, I had a question. I asked him what would happen to Soweto in a white homeland? What would happen to the blacks who live among us, like in Brits? He said we must not discuss that until the time comes. That was in 1962. We have a saying in Afrikaans, you mustn't go fetch the baboon on the other side of the mountain. That's what he was saying. Politicians don't answer the things that don't suit them."

"I resigned from the party then. At the time, there was no party to the right of the Nationalists. I had my own ideas. I didn't think I was in the wilderness; I thought I was in civilization, and everyone else was in the wilderness."

While at Pretoria, he met and married Yelena. Her father was a diamond cutter of German heritage. Her mother was an Afrikaner. Yelena grew up in Alberton, just south of Johannesburg.

After qualifying as a veterinarian, de la Rey took a job working for the state in South-West Africa, a sparsely populated territory then administered by South Africa and now known as Namibia. He worked in South-West for three years, but only one of them was for the government. After his first year, de la Rey started his own practice. It was a time of foot-and-mouth disease and as the only private veterinarian in the territory, he had to cover enormous distances. He acquired an old four-seater airplane and learned to fly it himself.

The post in South-West was never meant to be permanent. "My parents were living in Brits at the time," he recalls. "When I came to visit, I saw there was no veterinarian here, and I'd have more time for the family."

In Brits, de la Rey's practice grew steadily. He treated everything on four legs from Abyssinian cats to Aberdeen steers. "But it took a bit of time before they knew me. I played sports a lot when I first came. I played on five different rugby teams, and they had a hundred members, distributed quite widely among the population. I'd advise any chap who wants to start a practice in a small town to play sports."

He thought highly of the people. He respected their values, their solidity, their sense of responsibility. It was an Afrikaner town: English-speakers were few, and no one wanted more. "I liked the people of Brits," he says. "They are very conservative. I don't just mean politically, but in all respects. In areas like sex, education, drugs, religion. Everything. But I think country people all over the world are more conservative than city people. There is a sense of order here."

"Brits," he says, echoing the sentiment of many in town, "is a microcosm of South Africa."

THE TSWANA ARE A SOTHO-SPEAKING people of small, patrilineal communities who migrated into central South Africa in the fifteenth century. They farmed in the dark soil of the valley behind the Magaliesberg and hunted in the bushveld which teemed with game. In the nineteenth century, the Tswana were buffeted by the *Difaqane*, the Ngoni word for "crushing," a series of bloody conflicts among the black tribes in central South Africa. The Tswana were terrorized by the Matabele.

After the Voortrekkers annihilated the Matabele in the 1830s, forcing them to retreat to the western reaches of South Africa, the Tswana again lived in relative peace. But the Afrikaner and the

Tswana never trusted each other: the Tswana regarded the Boers as brutal and cold-blooded, and the Boers considered the Tswana lazy and duplicitous.

During the Anglo-Boer War, the Tswana sided with the British. They were easy converts for English missionaries and proved adept as messengers and scouts for the British army. After the English victory, the British military ceded to the Tswana the villages and cattle of the Makatese, a Sotho-speaking tribe who had aided the Boers during the war. The Tswana had hoped that a British victory might bring greater rights and opportunities, but the 1905 Native Affairs Commission favored strict territorial and political segregation of black and white.

Life's great-grandmother was a Makatese who married a Tswana after the war. They lived in a tiny village near the Crocodile River. Her son, Life's maternal grandfather, took the name Mfifi and became a builder, putting up one of the first houses in Oukasie in the 1920s. Life's mother remembers the house as number 167 Toka Street, right next to a Salvation Army church where every Sunday morning missionaries thumped out earnest marching music on an upright piano.

Mfifi had a specialty: thatched roofs. When Afrikaners first encountered the black tribes of the highveld, they were intrigued by their round, hive-shaped huts. The structures consisted of a light framework of woven saplings covered by a thick roof of grass thatching, supported by a single pole in the center. The thatching kept the hut cool in summer, warm in winter, and dry during the rainy season. The Afrikaners admired them and called them *rondawels*. In the 1930s, Life's grandfather fashioned many rondavels and thatched roofs for white houses in town.

Life's mother was born and raised in Oukasie. She attended a Dutch Reformed school, and learned English, Afrikaans, and Tswana. As a girl, she loved to go to the movies. Every Friday and Saturday night, the Roman Catholic hall showed films on a large white sheet. Admission was two shillings. American Westerns were the most popular pictures, but Mrs. Buys was partial to the comedies. She *adored* Laurel and Hardy. "I could have watched them forever," she says. The only shadow in their lives, she remembers, was the sense that someday they would have to move.

One day, when she was eighteen, she went to visit some friends in Pretoria. She began to feel ill and they took her to a local black clinic where she was treated and released. As she was leaving, a young, pleasant-looking man asked her if he could give her a ride. Where was she going? Brits, she replied. Well, it so happened that he was going there as well. Why didn't she come along?

Buys worked as a truck driver on a large farm fifteen kilometers outside Brits. Driving a truck was a prestigious job. The farmer trusted him, and Buys had a small house to himself on the farmer's property. Sometimes he would be away on a delivery for two or three days at a time.

Buys began to court Mfifi. He would pick her up in Oukasie and they would go for drives in the bushveld. But when he asked her to marry him, she hesitated. Buys was Coloured. His family came from the mixed-race community of Coloured at the Cape and had migrated north with a white farmer who had decided to try his luck in the Transvaal.

The Coloured, one of South Africa's four main racial categories, are sometimes known as "brown Afrikaners" because they are descended from mixed parentage and generally speak Afrikaans as their first language. Since "light-skinned" Coloured were virtually impossible to differentiate from Afrikaners, the Population Registration Act of 1950 emphasized association and ancestry as the principal ways of establishing who was white. The Cape Coloured, who formed a distinct community in the nineteenth century, tended to look down on rural blacks and the Mfifis were chary about their daughter marrying a Coloured man. In the end, her family relented and the two were wed.

They went to live on the farm and stayed in housing provided by the farmer. Mrs. Buys worked in the fields while her husband continued to drive. Marshall was their firstborn and spent his early years on the farm. When he was growing up, he used his mother's surname, Mfifi, so that he could go to black schools. Coloured children attended separate schools with the Indians.

Life remembers how hard his father worked. "The people on the farm worked from six A.M. till six P.M. My father often worked longer than that. He'd wake up at one A.M. and then he'd be off to Johannesburg delivering the farmer's goods. He drove all over the Reef. He'd come back at three or four in the afternoon, and then supervise the loading for the next day. He would always make sure that each child would have the best meal possible. If you didn't like the food, he would get in the truck and drive into town to buy something you liked."

When the farm was sold, Buys had a disagreement with the new owner and left. He moved to Oukasie and they lived in a shack on his wife's family's property.

"My father was cheeky," Life says. "He couldn't get along with the new owners. Once he got to Oukasie, he never worked. But he always wished to have things done right. When I was busy with him, all of my friends were too afraid to come and ask for me. He was a tough man. You wouldn't dare to be absent from school, because he would get very angry. He would say you should have some good meals so that you could study. One time I showed him how I spent only ten cents of the fifty he gave me for food. He was very angry. He said you couldn't study on an empty stomach."

School came easily to Life. He didn't need to study much. He was a hell-raiser, but the teachers said he had a silver tongue and could talk his way out of anything.

"I never thought about politics when I was young. Man, you think about making money!" Life raises his eyebrows and laughs. "Going to university. Driving a beautiful car. Not a limousine. I never thought about limousines. Not a Cadillac, either. Americans don't make good cars. A Mercedes. Yes, a Mercedes. Have my parents in a beautiful house. You know, building castles in the air.

"When I was young I thought I ought to become a civil engineer. But I don't like heights. Then you get to your real life, and you have to start carrying responsibilities. You learn it is not very easy. You get detained. You get fired. You get debts. Deaths in the family. Funerals cost a lot of money. You never prepare for death.

"You know, our teachers were telling us about the problems we were facing. It was all around. The white man is *baas*. My father lost his job, I could see that. We saw how we were treated."

Life's schooling was frequently interrupted. "When I was nineteen, there were the riots in Soweto about studying in Afrikaans. We felt we should show some kind of solidarity. We discussed it and decided to boycott classes until they agreed that there should be no Afrikaans in the school. But things turned out the other way around. Our school was burnt down and I was one of the people charged. I got eight lashes. The older students got sentenced to three years in prison. We got punished according to our ages." Life was kicked out of school and spent a month in detention.

Life returned to Oukasie. He wasn't working or studying. Later that year, he found out that his girlfriend was pregnant. He had heard that there were positions open at Firestone, and he was hired as a technical quality inspector. He took his matriculation exam while he was at Firestone in 1978, and passed. His son was born in July 1978. His girfriend became pregnant again in 1981, but decided to abort the child. She did not tell Life about her plan and died during the operation.

"She was a real chick-y, you know what I mean?" Life says. "She was kind of aggressive. She had reason to be that way. She was a very fine lady. Very clever, very intelligent. She was the best young lady in Brits. It took me about three years so that I could handle it. I lost something very valuable."

Life was never on good terms with her parents. They resented him because he had not married their daughter and treated him like a stranger. "I remember the very same day, I couldn't enter my in-laws' house—we went to Abel's house instead. Abel told me that life couldn't stop for the death of one person. I got drunk there that whole day and night. The next day I just continued drinking. I never drank the way I drank that day. I didn't want to give it a thought."

LURED BY RECRUITING AGENTS who conjured up streets paved with gold, Manilal Bhula left India in 1902 aboard a swarming steamship bound for Durban, on the eastern coast of South Africa. His first job after landing was as a stevedore on the docks. Like thousands of other freshly arrived Indians, he was soon beset with gold fever and went to work in the mines of the Reef. When he fulfilled his contract after three years, he had saved enough money to become a hawker. He went first to Potchefstroom and then Rustenburg, tramping from house to house with a basket of fruit and goods atop his head.

The Bhula family came from the Gujarat region on the west coast of India and were among the second wave of Indians who migrated to South Africa. Unlike most of those from Gujarat who sailed to South Africa, the Bhulas were Hindus. They were members of the Vaiśya, the class of traders and merchants, the third of the four Hindu castes. The majority of Indians who migrated to

South Africa came from the Vaiśya class and the one below it, the Sudra, or laboring class.

Jai's grandfather was born in Rustenburg and eventually opened a general store there. The Bhulas were the only Hindu family in town. Indians were restricted from owning property and, under the Transvaal Immigration Act of 1908, local authorities could refuse them trading licenses for any reason. Whereas some Indians in the area prospered, Mr. Bhula did not. The shop was bedeviled by robberies and customers were scarce.

One day, an Indian gentleman walked into Mr. Bhula's shop and made him a proposition. He told Bhula that he had been observing him for some time and found him to be an honorable man. The gentleman owned a tearoom in Brits, and he proposed that Mr. Bhula run it. He offered to pay half of Bhula's costs, and Bhula would receive a 5 percent royalty. Bhula could operate the place for as long as he wanted. Bhula agreed. The shop proved not much to look at (it was actually a *kafee,* the Afrikaans term for a simple café or coffee shop; tearoom was too genteel a description), but luck was with him. Not long after he took over, a bus stop was created in front of the *kafee* and business prospered.

Jai's mother was eight years old when the boat carrying her parents and five brothers and sisters arrived in Durban in 1946. The Mistry family had come from a remote village in Gujarat, and South Africa appeared miraculous to her. "It was a wonder," she remembers. "My father took me for a pair of shoes. It was my first pair of shoes. Until then I had only worn sandals. When I put them on, I couldn't look up. I walked around staring down at my shoes."

Her father was one of three brothers who owned businesses in India, Johannesburg, and Brits. Their custom was to take turns staying a year in each place. Her family spent their first year in Johannesburg and lived on the sixth floor of an apartment building in what is now Lenasia, the city's Indian area. On Sundays, they took drives to Brits. "We had American cars in those days," Mrs. Bhula recalls. "Buicks, Oldsmobiles. We used to pile the children into the car, sometimes twenty in one car." In Brits they stayed at her aunt's house and had picnics down by the river.

The family moved to Brits the following year where the brothers owned Savemore, a large general dealership on Tom Street. The store sold a bit of everything. Later, they bought Afrikan Bazaar, another general store a few doors down from Savemore. Both catered to the white laborers working on the Hartbeespoort Dam who could not afford to shop in the white stores.

The Mistry clan lived at number 30 Tom Street in a graceful colonial-style house with molded tin ceilings and a wide veranda with simple white columns. The house was set back from the street behind the entrance of the store. Palms shaded the small front yard. Inside they used simple Boer furniture. Next to the house, in a narrow barrackslike building, the brothers housed their black workers.

Mrs. Bhula beheld her husband's face for the first time at their wedding. Her marriage, like all marriages in Primindia, was arranged. Their union was negotiated by the fathers of the bride and the groom, who knew each other from business. Mrs. Bhula was twenty, Mr. Bhula, twenty-one.

"I did not talk to my husband for the first time until two days after the wedding," she remembers. "My father had said that he was getting old and wanted to see his daughters married before he died." She pauses, and adds, "My father is still alive."

Mrs. Bhula lived with her husband's family in a rondavel next to the railway line. "Oh, it was an immense change," she recalls. "So very, very different from the life I knew. I cried and cried for months." There was an open field around the house, she says, "and there were many huge jacarandas. They were so large that two people together couldn't reach around the trunk. When it rained, the flowers used to fall on the ground and cover the road. It was very *royal*. My father-in-law had a *kafee* so we used to have fresh fruit and vegetables. On Saturday evenings, we sometimes had cheese and tomato and banana sandwiches on thick bread that was still warm."

There were no facilities of any kind in Brits for Indians. No community center, no playground, no park. There was also no public transport for non-whites, so a car was necessary to go anywhere. The Bhulas sometimes drove into Pretoria and passed the white playgrounds in town. Mrs. Bhula remembers trying to distract Jai's attention so that he would not ask her why he couldn't play there.

Tom Street was Jai's playground. For Jai and his friends, the dusty, dirt road became their cricket pitch, and the narrow passageways between the buildings formed their soccer goals. They played cowboys and Indians in the vacant yards behind the shops. Jai went swimming for the first time on Tom Street in the enormous vat that the blacksmith used to cool hot iron. After the blacksmith had gone for the day, the children would clamber up the side and leap into the water.

In 1957, the owner of the *kafee* where Mr. Bhula's father worked decided he wanted it back. He was reneging on his promise, but Mr. Bhula did not protest. "My father gave it back to him," Jai says. "My father was a very honest man. He would say, your books must be clean. He did not believe in insurance. He said, if your books are clean, the shop will never burn down."

The following year, Jai's father and his brother, who used the surname Prema, opened a general store on Kruis Street. Kruis Street was regarded as a backwater; anything off Tom Street was considered a hopeless location. But the shop benefited from an action taken by the white Town Council which galled the Indian merchants: the council voted to cut off Tom Street as the principal entrance to Brits. They did not want whites to have to enter the town through an Indian area. Kruis Street was now the main artery for traffic from the white town to enter Primindia.

Jai's childhood was sunny and mild. His small world was bounded by the railway line. "I don't think I even knew what apartheid was when I was growing up in Brits," Jai says. "But it was clear that whites did not like us. People had been beaten up for crossing the railway."

He was an excellent student and eventually became head prefect of his school. Politics were a distant rumble. "I don't know the moment when I became political. I know most certainly that when I was about twelve, I became aware of some things. I had a teacher whom I remember respecting very much. There was a sign in calligraphy to his right, and it said, 'Let truthfulness be the anchor of your life.' He never discussed politics as such. But he had a close friend, a high-school teacher who died in detention. That made an impression.

"I was aware of the hostility of whites toward blacks and Coloureds and Indians. I used to see my father referring to whites in— how should I say it?—he referred to them with awe and undue respect. To an old white man, he would say, *Oubaas,* and to a woman, he would say *Missus.* On occasion he was actually abusive toward blacks, which I found repugnant.

"In high school, politics were taboo. People shied away from it. My schooldays were in the aftermath of the treason trial. There was a great amount of fear. 'Don't get involved in politics' was the attitude. I read the newspaper quite heavily in high school, so I knew something of what was going on.

"I was head prefect in standard nine and ten. The prefects are seen as authoritarian. They're appointed by staff and the principal. It would be better to have students elect their own representatives, but at that time it was all so new. We were supposed to stand at the gate and if people came late, we were to report them to the principal. In my two years I never took anyone to the office. On May 31, Republic Day, we were told to raise the flag. But I refused. Republic Day is no cause to celebrate. I don't see it as a day that inspires patriotism. That day is still to be decided. I think in my high-school years, I was known for being outspoken. To stand up against apartheid, that is not politics, but it was viewed as so."

Jai's graduating class was the first in which anyone from Primindia went to university. Boys generally graduated from high school and went to work for their fathers in the shop. But Jai applied to the University of Witwatersrand in Johannesburg, one of the premier English-speaking universities in South Africa, and was accepted. Jai's father had mixed emotions: he was proud of his son, but thought that a university education might make him too high-and-mighty to work in the shop.

Jai decided he wanted to be an architect and enrolled in design. He also got involved in student politics. "The things I did at university were very small, inconsequential. Minor acts of conscience. I never thought I should be doing more. Or that I should be doing less."

He had one term remaining in his final year when his father died. Jai felt he had to return home, that his place was with his mother and sister. He believed that his responsibility was to look after the family by taking over his father's share in the shop. Mrs. Bhula offered to work in the shop herself, so that Jai could get his degree, but Jai's uncle objected. He wanted a man behind the counter.

"When my father died," Jai says, "I felt very strongly about what I should do. I wanted to come and work in the shop. I felt that way as head of the family. I didn't want the apple cart to be upset. I was willing to put the shop in my mother's name and just work there. But my uncle did not want to take chances on her being in the shop. So we put it in my name."

He figured that when things settled down, he would fulfill his commitments to the university and get his degree. Jai never planned on working in the shop; he went to university so that he would not have to.

For Jai, the shop always symbolized what his father stood for and what he rejected. "When I was younger, I told my father that there was absolutely nothing he could do to get me in the shop. And then he did the one and only thing that could get me in the shop. He passed away."

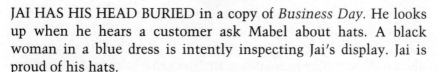

JAI HAS HIS HEAD BURIED in a copy of *Business Day*. He looks up when he hears a customer ask Mabel about hats. A black woman in a blue dress is intently inspecting Jai's display. Jai is proud of his hats.

"I think I have the best range in town," he says.

Many of them are fanciful: pillboxes with flowers, toques with plumes, wide-brimmed fedoras. He likes the combination of extravagant design and severe color. "I think hats look best in black and white," he says. "I always order hats in black and white."

Hats are something new for Bhula Prema and Sons. "We used to not sell hats," Jai says. "Where we now have hats, we sold skin-lightening creams. But when I joined the shop, I told my uncle that I did not want to work here if the shop sold such products."

The customer points to a hat that looks like a banana split, long and yellow with a cherry on top. She plunks it on her head, regards herself in the mirror, frowns, adjusts it, and then smiles.

"I have a headache," she says. "Maybe this hat will help. I think it will make me *happy*," she says, as she reaches into her high heels for the cash.

A very bourgeois-looking black woman in a narrow-brimmed black hat walks in. It's not one of Jai's. She looks around, but seems to have a sniffy attitude about the merchandise. It doesn't look as if she will find anything. Mabel just stands next to her as she peruses things.

She picks up a denim skirt with a small American flag sewn on the pocket. The flag has only a few stars and half-a-dozen stripes.

"This," she says, and places it on the counter.

"Would you like shoes to go with it?" Jai asks.

She half nods. Maybe.

"Low heel? Medium heel or three-fourths?" Jai asks.

"Medium," she says, expressionless. She looks up and down, back and forth, across the rows of shoes. Jai uses a yardstick to point to shoes along the wall like a teacher directing attention to a theorem on the blackboard.

"We have this one," Jai says. "This one is nice."

The woman is unmoved. Afterward, Mabel tells Jai that the woman was from Lethlabile. Jai says the more sophisticated black customer comes from a city or town and prefers muted colors. Blacks from the country favor louder colors, reds, yellows, turquoise. A city woman associates bright colors with farm workers, hayseeds. Anything bright is said to *shout*. "That dress shouts," she might say. The more urban the woman, the more Western her taste.

Jai finds it remarkable how quickly a style becomes popular. It seems to happen overnight. At the moment, denim rules. Jai has denim dresses, denim pants, denim hats, denim jackets—all kinds of denim, distressed, stone-washed, tie-dyed. Anything "American" jumps off the shelves. Many of the product labels are red, white, and blue with stars and stripes on them, as though it were some kind of official U.S.A. seal of approval. All are made in South Africa.

Jai is in the storeroom when he hears Afrikaans being spoken out front. He walks to the counter. A middle-aged white woman asks, in Afrikaans, whether he has a particular type of children's shoe with a strap across the top. Jai pauses for a moment and replies, in English, "Do you want boys or girls?"

"Vir my dogter," she answers.

"No, we don't," Jai says evenly.

"Dankie," she replies, and breezes out.

When white, Afrikaans-speaking customers come into the shop—not a frequent occurrence—Jai stiffens. On the surface, he acts indifferent. But he is on guard.

If the white customer addresses him in Afrikaans, as they invariably do, he answers in English. "Sometimes the Afrikaner comes in and he is so haughty and proud," Jai says. "I know that he does not consider me a South African, but a foreigner, yet he insists, he *demands* that I speak Afrikaans. He wants it both ways. So when he starts speaking in Afrikaans in my shop, I will sometimes say, 'Excuse me, what are you saying?' and make him speak English. But if they come in and are old, I will talk to them in Afrikaans. Or if a black comes in who speaks to me in Afrikaans I will talk to him in Afrikaans."

English is a foreign language in Brits and English speakers are still treated like *uitlanders,* the pejorative term for "foreigners" used by the Boers before the war. English-speaking South Africans, the descendants of nineteenth-century British colonists, make up 36 percent of the whites in South Africa, but less than 10 percent of the whites in Brits. Traditionally, the Afrikaners have dominated the politics of South Africa, while the English speakers ruled the economy. The Afrikaners of Brits still bear some resentment toward English speakers—who are always referred to as "English"—and insinuate that they have dual loyalties, to Britain and South Africa.

Jai is competent in Afrikaans, but not truly fluent. He knows the words, but not the music. "I myself don't have an Afrikaans turn of phrase. I speak it in a very bookish way. I don't use the correct idioms." Jai took Afrikaans for seven years in school, but it was always a chore. Nowadays students in Primindia question why they have to learn Afrikaans, but not when Jai was head prefect.

"Brits students were regarded as absolutely brilliant at Afrikaans," he says. "I remember a girl from our school went to Durban to study. She wasn't that good in Afrikaans, but when she went there her Afrikaans was even better than the teacher's. By the same token, English was not terribly good here in Brits. Some of my early school friends are still not very fluent in English. Perhaps they are just not very articulate, I don't know. But you still find people my age who speak to each other in Afrikaans.

"Today it's absolutely anomalous to hear an Indian child speaking Afrikaans. You never hear it. It's too bad in a way. You know, Afrikaans has some very good poetry. The poetry has so much humanness in it. But now the language has taken on the symbolism of oppression."

· · ·

Bhula Prema and Sons does not depend on white customers. Nearly all their traffic is black. Jai's manner with white customers is chilly; his uncle verges on the obsequious.

"I wouldn't say I even really know any white people," he says. "The Afrikaner is a strange race. There is some intangible, undefinable quality that they all seem to have. *Skelm*—it's a kind of dull-witted shrewdness. It is very small, but they all have it. The Afrikaner is like a dog who has been kicked too often and is mean and scared and shrewd.

"He is so emphatic about his culture. About his language, his history, his symbols. It is a sign of insecurity. We do not go around saying we have a culture that is four thousand years old. The white idea of racial purity is a strange notion to me. I don't really understand it. Race is a set of circumstances. I can see value in culture, but not in race. The Afrikaner thinks race and culture are the same thing. There is no such thing as racial purity anyway. A book last year even pointed out that Andries Treurnicht [the leader of the Conservative party] had a Coloured ancestor."

Jai particularly resents—though he is sometimes guilty of it himself—the way whites make generalizations about Indians and blacks. "I find that whites believe they think individually, but that blacks and Indians think en masse. They will also say, 'My domestic told me that she is afraid of opposing sanctions because she will be attacked in the township.' From that they think they know how blacks are really feeling. 'Of course,' " and his voice turns sarcastic, " 'she is not afraid to tell me these things because she knows I am her friend.'

"Most white South Africans know more about what is going on in Lebanon than their own backyard. They probably know more about what goes on in Europe than in Oukasie. It is in part because of the restricted media, which shows only what the government wants people to see. But people here only see what they want to see. When you hear white political leaders make a plea for unity among South Africans, a foreigner might think, Ah, what lofty sentiments, but actually all they are talking about is unity between Afrikaans-speaking South Africans and English-speaking South Africans. The whites don't even see the blacks as part of the equation."

Whites, he says, are always talking about the different black tribes; how the Zulu is as dissimilar to the Tswana as the white is to the Indian. "Whites always say look at the rest of Africa, as though all Africa were one. Few have ever traveled in Africa anyway; most countries won't allow them in. But in South Africa the whites always say look how many different tribes there are. But then they point to Africa as if it's all one tribe. It's only the minority that thinks in terms of groups and races. The majority simply regard themselves as South African. I'm proud to be part of that majority. To the minority, it is simply the way things are done and the way they have always been done. To the majority, it is oppression."

Whites assert that they are superior, Jai notes, but how could one ever know since they have skewed the situation in their favor. Jai mentions that the government recently rescinded the last of the job reservation laws, which required that all elevator operators be white. "It was created to guarantee that no white would ever be in an inferior position to a black." Jai finds a touch of the absurd in this. "If they really believed they were better," he says, "would it be necessary to create laws guaranteeing social, monetary, and political superiority?"

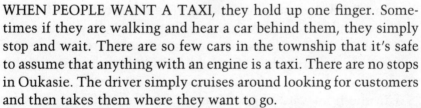

WHEN PEOPLE WANT A TAXI, they hold up one finger. Sometimes if they are walking and hear a car behind them, they simply stop and wait. There are so few cars in the township that it's safe to assume that anything with an engine is a taxi. There are no stops in Oukasie. The driver simply cruises around looking for customers and then takes them where they want to go.

Life pulls over for two elderly women, both of whom are holding tattered umbrellas as parasols against the sun. They climb slowly into the taxi and take seats in the middle of the three narrow rows behind Life. They tell him that they are going to town to do some grocery shopping on Murray Avenue. Where? Checkers, they say. More and more, Life has noticed, the women of Oukasie are doing their grocery shopping in the big supermarkets in the white area; the prices are cheaper and the selection wider than in Primindia where they traditionally shopped. The white merchants are trying to lure back the black customers they once consigned to the Indians.

"Hey, big boy!" Life calls out to a hefty fellow by the side of the road. The man smiles, and yells back, "Hey, Life!" As he drives, Life will lean out the window and say, *"Eh ta?"* or "How's it?" People smile and call back either *"Tcha"* or "Fine." When people say, "How's it?" to him, he often replies, "Lekker, lekker," the Afrikaans word for "Sweet" or "nice."

Lekker is one of only a handful of Afrikaans words that blacks use in everyday speech. Life only speaks Afrikaans under duress, though he says he is more eloquent in it than English. If he is addressed by a white in Afrikaans, he answers in Afrikaans. Life's father spoke the language at home; Life learned English in school. English is the language everyone wants to speak, and Life wishes he spoke it better. It is, he says with a smile, the language of liberation.

Life drives with jaunty abandon. A woman signals him to stop and asks him whether he would pick up a six-pack of Castle for her. "Sure," Life says. Another woman stops Life and tells him that if he runs into her daughter to tell her that she will be home in the afternoon. Life nods. "Sure." The taxi driver is a mobile switchboard for a town with no telephones; he takes and gives messages, imparts news, relays gossip.

Oukasie may not have street names, but it does have neighborhoods. Greenside, whose lanes Life is now rumbling down, used to be considered the sticks of Oukasie. The old people recall Greenside as a kind of Eden. Now it is densely settled with shanties; only a few of the original houses from forty years ago remain. As Life maneuvers the taxi, the side of the car is sometimes just inches from the shacks it is passing.

In the front yard of one shack, a man is sitting in a wooden chair getting a haircut. The fellow waves to Life and calls out, *"Dumela."* The barber has a pair of oversized shears which look comical when compared to the stubble of hair on the man's head. In Oukasie, life is lived outdoors. Indoors, there is little light and less room, so people in Oukasie do outdoors what others in Brits do indoors. People wash themselves, eat and drink, and carry on in their front yards. If a husband and wife fight, they often do it in front of their house. Everyone knows everyone else's business. The reason for the dearth of privacy is both economic and cultural; people can't afford it, but don't seem to feel deprived without it.

. . .

Life drives across a small bridge. The canal it passes over feeds
the Crocodile River. In heavy rain, the tunnel sometimes becomes clogged and a pond is formed by backed-up water.
Then children scamper out to play in the township's newest swimming hole.

Before the drought, people bathed in the canal and drank from
it. Many of the residents developed bilharzia as a result. Bilharzia
is a freshwater-borne disease carried by snails in which parasitic
worms bore into the bladder and intestines causing internal bleed-
ing. It is still not uncommon among children in Oukasie, though
non-existent among whites.

This morning, there are about a dozen men, bare to the waist,
trying to gouge out a new passageway for the water. The idea was
put forth by the Brits Action Committee, the local group which has
taken the place of the community councillors, now that they have
all moved to Lethlabile. Life is head of the Action Committee.

There is an abundance of manpower around the bridge, but an
absence of organization. Life gets out of the taxi to investigate. Two
men are standing in the stream, wielding picks. Behind them children are splashing in the water. Life walks down to the water and
motions for one of the fellows to hand him a pick. He literally rolls
up his sleeves, and begins to hack away at the wall. After no more
than a dozen swings, he yells for the fellow to come back and
relieve him of the pick. He smiles sheepishly. By temperament,
Life is a supervisor, not a worker. He very much wants people to
think that he is industrious, but no one really does.

The Action Committee believes it is important for the people
of Oukasie to show that they care about their township. There have
been other cleanup projects, but this is the first time that anyone
has tried to fix the tunnel. Life cannot recall who first made the
suggestion to repair the tunnel.

"It was everyone's idea," he says.

In Oukasie, the notion that an idea has a single father is considered a form of vanity. Ideas are everyone's. No one, not even Life
—who is not always modest—will claim credit for being the origi-
nator of an idea. "We share ideas," he says. By definition, an idea is
good if everyone agrees to it. Consensus is necessary *and* sufficient.
One reason even the simplest meeting in Oukasie take so long is
that everyone has to concur before anything is settled. As with a
jury, the verdict must be unanimous.

· · ·

Life drives northeast toward Vuka. Vuka is short for the Zulu phrase Vuka U'Sezensele, which roughly translated means, "Wake up, and do something for yourself." Twenty years ago, Vuka was the most remote part of the township. Vuka is up a steep hill and is the highest point in Oukasie. People moved to Vuka from the more congested areas at the bottom. The first settlers were considered pioneers.

"Another reason it is called Vuka," Life says, "is because there were lots of Xhosa people who stayed there. They lived in compounds. They were very aggressive. In 1957, they were instrumental in organizing a bus boycott. There had been an increase in the bus fare. They went up and down the township and made sure the people did not ride in the buses."

Today, Vuka is as crowded as the rest of the township. But it still has a sense of openness about it. The air smells fresher. Just on the other side of the bridge that leads to Vuka is the Oukasie soccer ground, a patchy, rolling field, more dirt than grass. A couple of boys, each with their right shoe off, are kicking a deflated soccer ball back and forth. Soccer is the most popular sport in the township. In the past, the field had been used almost every night for soccer games. But when the township was "abolished," the white Administration Board removed the goalposts and announced that if the people of Oukasie wanted to play soccer, they could do so at the new field in Lethlabile.

Life lingers at the soccer field for a moment—he says he was a "very tricky" player in his time—and then looks around for riders. There are none.

Life turns to the right at the northernmost border of Vuka, and on his left passes the township's principal graveyard. The graves are all aboveground, most covered with stone or brick. Weeds and tall grass thrive between the plots. Many of the gravestones have been knocked over. The ones left standing are inscribed mainly in Tswana, though quite a few are in Zulu. The inscriptions are simple: R NTSOENG . . . 1916 . . . RIP. Some of the stones are made of a distinctive speckled granite, once known as Brits Granite. The granite was given to the families of the black laborers who worked in the local quarries. Until the 1960s, Brits was the granite capital of South Africa, producing a third of the Republic's supply.

Catty-corner to the black graveyard is the Coloured one. The blacks of Oukasie don't want any Coloured in their graveyard. The

Coloured cemetery is far neater than the black one and has recently been swept. The headstones are larger and more elaborate. Some are two-tiered like wedding cakes or shaped like hearts or scrolls. Red and white plastic mums in simple vases decorate many of the graves. The headstones are all inscribed in Afrikaans: WILLEMSE. HIER RUS ONS DIERBARE OUERS EN GROOTOUERS. (Willemse. Here rest our beloved parents and grandparents.)

The Coloured graveyard in Oukasie is part of what is known as Noodcamp, Afrikaans for "Emergency Camp." Noodcamp is where Brits's Coloured live. They number about 550. Noodcamp was officially declared a Coloured area only in 1970, but Coloured families had been living there for thirty years.

Under South Africa's racial classifications, Coloured and black are separate categories. South Africa's 2.8 million Coloured population, 85 percent of whom live in the Cape Province, formed a distinct community at the Cape in the nineteenth century. For generations, the Coloured found themselves in a middle position in the racial hierarchy. With the enactment of the first round of apartheid laws in the early 1950s, they were forced to live in their own Group Areas and abide by the manifold restrictions of petty apartheid regulations. The Group Areas Act displaced many thousands of Coloured who were living in urban areas that were declared exclusively white.

The Coloured here are mainly descendants of servants who had journeyed north to the Transvaal to work for white families. When the old mill was put up near the Crocodile River, many Coloured families who had been living there as squatters were displaced. At that time, the Town Council bought more land at the top of the Old Location and informed the Coloured to move there. They were told that Noodcamp was only temporary and that a more permanent place would be found. The government now says it has found an area for the Coloured. It is an empty swatch of bushveld about fifteen kilometers northeast of Brits which the authorities have named Damonsville. ("In South Africa," Life says, "the white man has names for places where there are no places.") Many of the Coloured were eager to move to Lethlabile, but were not allowed: Lethlabile is for blacks only. For the Coloured, Damonsville is their promised land.

The Coloured are part of Oukasie, but not of it. Coloured and black don't mix much. There are few marriages between the two groups. No one from Noodcamp serves on any of the committees in Oukasie. The Coloured feel frozen out, and are both resentful and puzzled. Many blacks in Oukasie think the Coloured cannot be trusted. The Coloured, they say, are too friendly with the white man. Some of the Coloured claim they would like to get more involved in the township, but they are afraid if they do so the government will backtrack on its promise to build them a place of their own. Life, despite having a Coloured father, has nothing to do with the Coloured community.

Life rolls through Noodcamp. The houses are better-con-structed and handsomer than those of Oukasie. Many are painted pastel colors: pink and pale green. Gardens are plentiful. The Coloured population contains a large number of artisans, many of whom work on construction crews in town. Even whites concede that the Coloured are the best artisans in the Transvaal. But the craftsmen of Noodcamp scoff at the houses they have built here. They say that if Noodcamp was not temporary, they would have built homes to be proud of.

As a rule, Life doesn't pick up passengers in Noodcamp. None of the drivers do. The dirt road passes through Noodcamp and then narrows as it traverses about fifty meters of bushveld and then comes out on a well-paved road in Elandsrand, the new white de-velopment.

Elandsrand is the ritziest area of Brits. It was conceived in the early 1970s after Brits was designated by the government as a so-called border industry area. Elandsrand was designed to house all the upscale industrialists who would be coming to town.

In many places, Oukasie is less than a hundred meters from Elandsrand. The proximity is unusual. Although nearly all white towns in South Africa have a satellite black township, few towns in South Africa are like Brits with town and township side by side. Traditionally, townships were built close enough to allow black labor to commute, but distant enough that the life of the two towns did not impinge on each other. But in Brits, the township was never relocated and the white town expanded northward until it bumped up against the township.

Life remembers when Elandsrand was just a barren hillside. Another no-man's-land with a name. "This place was called Elandsfontein before anyone lived here. And then when they started building, people began asking why the white man was building up here. Why not build elsewhere?" Life shakes his head. It is inevitable, he says, that if the white man builds this close to the black man, the black man will have to go. "They do not want to be near us," he says.

Life pauses at the stop sign at the top of the hill, the highest point in Brits. From this vantage point, he surveys the town and township spread out before him. "Oukasie is the most prestigious place, eh?" he says, with a smile, and then accelerates down the hill toward town.

THE TOWN HALL, DE LA REY SAYS, is the most beautiful building in Brits. "When I think of Brits," he says, "I don't think of the churches, or the stores, or my lab. I see that old Town Hall."

The building forms a T-junction at the northern end of Murray Avenue, the main shopping street in what is known as the CBD— the Central Business District. The footprint of the building is in the shape of a laager—a reference to the circle of ox wagons at Blood River, the most sacred ground in Afrikaner history where, in 1838, a few hundred Voortrekkers vanquished a Zulu army of 12,000. The architect, de la Rey notes, was a scholar of North African design and the building has a definite Moorish sensibility. The graceful central tower has been built with a slight entasis, a convex curve which prevents the illusion of hollowness if the sides are straight. Completed in 1949, it is anticolonial architecture and one of the few interesting buildings in town. Other than the Town Hall, the architecture of Brits is mostly charm-free, a collection of one-story concrete boxes with cheap plastic facades.

The building, de la Rey notes, is curiously situated. During the 1940s, Brits was developing in a northern direction, but the mayor of the town owned property to the east. He decided to build the town hall perpendicular to Murray Avenue, which halted growth to the north and hastened it to the east.

De la Rey is in town to run an errand. He swings past the Town Hall and turns right on Murray Avenue. De la Rey does not enjoy going to town. He'd just as soon avoid it. He thinks the shops sell a lot of rubbish to uneducated black consumers and witless white ones. He looks for a parking space in front of the post office, which is just across the street from the Town Hall. The trick is to find a space in the shade. Cars parked in the sun turn into four-wheeled saunas. Most farmers, like de la Rey, have lamb's wool covering on the seats to prevent the leather from baking. People always lock their doors when in town.

Inside the post office a dozen or so white women are mailing letters and a few black men are buying stamps. De la Rey nods at one of the ladies. They wear light sleeveless dresses and have large dimpled shoulders. Not much jewelry, perhaps a gold chain around the neck. Digital watches are de rigueur. Eye shadow tends toward the edges of the spectrum: purple, magenta, turquoise. Toes are crammed into sandals that are too tight and too high—some have inch-and-a-half heels. The women are not light on their feet. Their element is earth, not air.

One street northeast of the post office is where the town's cinema used to be. It closed three years ago, and is now the Full Gospel Church, an offshoot of the fundamentalist American Church of God, which practices speaking in tongues and originated in Cleveland, Tennessee, at the turn of the century. A mural of the Crucifixion covers a wall that once advertised coming attractions of a different kind.

Just behind the post office is the town's Wimpy Bar, Brits's first taste of American-style fast food. The Wimpy Bar is an English chain that modeled itself after McDonald's and Burger King. It is a bright, cheerful place with a color scheme of red, white, and blue. When the Wimpy opened, hamburgers were exotic fare in Brits. Especially the concoctions contained on the Wimpy menu such as the Hawaiian Burger (mayonnaise and a slice of pineapple) and something called the Jive Burger (lettuce, tomato, and hot sauce).

From the moment it opened in 1984, the Wimpy was the place to go for Brits's gilded youth. Every afternoon, it spilled over with Brits High School students in their maroon and gray uniforms sipping milk shakes and munching fries. The girls ladled on eye shadow and lipstick before going in; makeup in school is forbidden. Morné de la Rey went a few times, and developed a taste for hamburgers.

Last year, at the direction of Wimpy International, which is based in London, the local establishments in South Africa became "open" and permitted non-whites to eat there. Wimpy South Africa is a franchise of the British company and still takes direction from the home office. Many white parents were perturbed and ordered their children not to go. Soon blacks started eating at the Wimpy and the white clientele dwindled further. De la Rey is not against "open" restaurants, he simply won't patronize them. He prefers establishments like Brits's one French restaurant, Célèbre, which post RIGHT OF ADMISSION RESERVED signs in the window.

Driving down Murray Avenue he passes Travolta's Take-Aways, a popular *kafee* among young people because it has a video game. "A Greek *kafee*," de la Rey calls it. Inside, a barefoot, towheaded boy stands on his toes to see the video screen as an older, barefoot black boy plays Miss Pac-Man. Afrikaans kids, like black kids, walk barefoot in town. Morné remembers that his feet were like leather until he was fourteen, which is the time that white boys start wearing shoes.

All the *kafees* in Brits are run by Greeks or Portuguese immigrants. De la Rey believes such white immigrants to South Africa are useful. They take the jobs other whites won't do and blacks can't do legally. What disturbs him, though, is how few of them decide to become South African citizens. Most of the Greeks and Portuguese who live in Brits retain their citizenship in the country of their birth. "If an immigrant wants to stay here," de la Rey says, "he should be loyal to South Africa—otherwise, he can bugger off. If the Greek thinks of Greece as home, then I am very much more for the black man than for the Greek."

Whites in Brits, when referring to someone who is not an Afrikaner, always specify the person's ethnic origin. "If a new store or restaurant opens in town," says de la Rey, "we would say the Greek who opened the store or the Portuguese who opened the *kafee*. We say the German who does this or the Jew who does that."

In Brits, people are always identified by their differentness. The South African myth of nationhood is a kind of anti-melting pot. Each ethnic group seeks to preserve its own "identity." Assimilation is neither pursued nor wanted.

"It comes from apartheid," de la Rey says. "I think the idea of apartheid makes you more aware of the differences between people than the similarities. It's in our subconscious. But we like it that way. Everyone keeps their own identity."

· · ·

Just off Murray Avenue de la Rey passes Brits's old synagogue, a simple whitewashed shed with Doric columns. Today, it is a temple of sport, the home of the town's wrestling club. Built in 1928, it served the town's twenty or so Jewish families through the 1940s. Only four Jewish families remain in Brits: those of Dr. Friedland and his son, who is also a doctor; and the Lakier brothers, Nathan and Charlie, who own Drieir's, the town's largest hardware store. The Jews left Brits for several reasons: some moved because the town had no English schools, some left due to a lack of opportunities, and some were driven away by prejudice. The younger Dr. Friedland remembers that as a boy he was called a "bloody Jew" by the Afrikaner children and was once heckled off a school bus. Nathan Lakier's eldest son emigrated to America after he discovered that his own children were regularly taunted at the Brits elementary school. He now runs a health club in Dallas.

De la Rey has shopped at Drieir's for many years, and respects Nathan Lakier. Lakier is in his seventies and speaks Afrikaans with a raspy, Yiddish accent. He chain-smokes filterless cigarettes in the style of the 1930s, holding them between thumb and forefinger.

"You know, there was a large community of Jews before the war," recalls Lakier. "Nearly forty. Anyway, the anti-Semitism started during the war. This area, however, was pro-German. The mayor booted all the Jews off the Chamber of Commerce."

But Lakier insists that the old days were better days. "A few years ago, you knew everybody. You couldn't walk down the street without shaking hands. Couldn't pass by a farmhouse without being invited in for tea. But, man, these bloody foreigners are hypocrites. This word apartheid. It should never have been created. We lived in peace with the black man. When Dr. Verwoerd came to power, he preached separateness. It was never an issue before. It's only that word."

As de la Rey drives past a pair of clothing stores at the southern end of Murray Avenue, he says matter-of-factly, "Indians own them." Non-whites are prevented by law from owning property in the Central Business District. But there is a way around the restrictions, and it is known as the nominee system.

It works like this. The white seller and the Indian buyer agree on a price for the property—which sometimes includes a cut of future profits for the white. Then they form a dummy corporation in which 51 percent of the stock is owned by the white partner. Thus the title appears to be in the name of a company which is white-owned. The white seller signs an undated letter of resignation from the company. If the Indian grows unhappy with his partner, he puts a date on the resignation letter.

In Brits, many Indian businessmen have the desire for land in the CBD and the cash to pay for it; many whites have the desire to sell and the need for cash. De la Rey estimates that as much as 40 or 50 percent of the CBD is owned by Indians through the nominee system. De la Rey mentions that some of the whites who have acted as nominees for Indian buyers have been political conservatives like himself. To him, they are hypocrites who are selling themselves down the river.

"Brown Jews." That is how whites describe the Indian merchants of Brits. The Indian, they say, is shrewd like the Jew; he will sell you woolen blankets when it's sweltering and bathing trunks when it's freezing. He bamboozles the black man, while posing as his friend. He puts his family to work for him, and makes them toil long hours.

The Jewish analogy has a subtler turn in that the whites believe that the Indian, like the Jew, has divided loyalties. While the Jew looks to Israel, the Indian pines for India. The whites see Indians driving BMWs and Mercedes and resent it. They especially distrust the Indians who are truckling to whites; they consider them two-faced—kowtowing to whites in public, mocking them in private.

"I'm much more for the black man than for the Indian," de la Rey says. "I feel the blacks have been here for many, many years. This is their home, this is their country, just like it is for me. Indians, however, are recent immigrants, and have the added disadvantage of not being Christians. They also have their own apartheid with the blacks. If you're a black here, you've lived here your whole life. If you're not satisfied, where shall you go? Many Indians still have ties with India and send their money there. The part the blacks have played in the development of this country is huge. The Indians don't deliver a big service to this country. You'll only find them in shops. Indians can only trade; they can't *work*."

ON THE CORNER, just down from Bhula Prema and Sons, half-a-dozen black boys are lollygagging in front of an electronics store smoking cigarettes and drinking Cokes. Michael Jackson's "Man in the Mirror" blasts from inside the shop. Michael Jackson, they say, is "number one."

As it nears midday, Primindia comes to life. A train leaving the station sends forth a resounding honk. Black workers swinging plastic bags filled with vegetables trudge back and forth across the railway line. Indian shop owners patrol the front of their establishments, scrutinizing how their rivals are faring. Men, in knee-length white shirts and embroidered skullcaps called "Topies," make their way to the mosque on Crocodile Street.

A truck pulls up in front of International Bag Buyers on Tom Street and black workers begin to unload wooden crates. Owned by the Tayob brothers, wealthy Indian businessmen, International Bag Buyers is Primindia's outstanding success story. In the 1940s, old man Tayob was a Muslim hawker who bought used, jute feed bags from local farmers, cleaned them, and sold them back at a profit. The business grew, but it didn't have a name. When he purchased a used van at Drieir's from Nathan Lakier which had the words INTERNATIONAL VAN stenciled on the side, Tayob simply painted BAG BUYERS over the latter word. The Tayob brothers now have a factory near Sun City that manufactures over a million polypropylene bags a month. The youngest brother just broke ground for a three-story house in the new extension in Primindia. The plans outline an indoor squash court, a sauna, Jacuzzi, and a glass-enclosed cupola for praying.

Across the way from Bhula Prema and Sons, the Transvaal Fish Shop begins to fill with black workers. They sit at cracked Formica tables eating chips, heavy on the salt and vinegar. The sign outside advertises CHIPS/PAP/VLEIS/FISH/VIENNAS/RUSSIANS. Pap is a porridge made from maize that is the staple of the local black diet (no meal is considered complete without it); vleis is Afrikaans for meat; Viennas are small, red sausages that look and taste like hot dogs; Russians are slightly larger sausages made from pork.

The shop is owned and run by Mr. Fong and his son. Mr. Fong, the last Chinese resident of Brits, resembles a caricature of a Chinaman from a Charlie Chan movie: hunched shoulders, wispy mustache, tiny glasses. His son, by contrast, has shoulder-length hair, wears Hawaiian shirts, and gives the impression he'd rather be at a disco. Mr. Fong's father came to South Africa from the Shantung province in China in the early 1900s. Along with nearly 50,000 Chinese, he had been recruited to work as a miner when there was a shortage of black labor after the Anglo-Boer War. Most of the Chinese were repatriated by 1910.

In addition to their *kafee*, Mr. Fong and his son operate a sideline. All day long, black customers hand Mr. Fong pieces of paper with numbers scribbled on them and some cash. The Fongs run the local Fah-fee enterprise, an ancient Chinese game of chance popular in townships throughout South Africa. There are thirty-six numbers, each of which stands for an object. Number 1 is a king or a lion, number 5 is a tiger, number 30 is a priest, and so on. If perchance you dream about a tiger, you bet number 5 the next day. A winning number returns approximately ten times the amount wagered.

Mr. Fong is not a gambling man himself. "I was born in Pretoria in 1917," Mr. Fong says. "My birth certificate was written in English and High Dutch. In those days, you didn't want to go outside. The Boers swore at us. They called us bananas: yellow on the outside, white on the inside. I tell you, we are civilized. We have a thousand years of civilization behind us. You can kill me, I don't care. But if you shame me—that is not good."

In 1949, Mr. Fong bought a shop from an Afrikaner which was located north of the railway line. "There were three Chinese families here when I first came to Brits," Mr. Fong says. "I was already here in 1952, when the Group Areas Act went into effect. The railway was supposed to divide Europeans from non-Europeans." Since the Chinese were then classified as Coloured, Mr. Fong was forced to sell his shop because it was in a white area. He was only reimbursed for the store, not the land. Despite his age, his anger seems unsoftened. In 1984, the minister of community development declared that the Chinese would henceforth have the status of "honorary whites" and would be allowed to own property in white areas without having to apply for permits. It was much too late for Mr. Fong.

He now lives in Pretoria and commutes the fifty kilometers to

Brits. "You know," Mr. Fong says, "there used to be Jews in this town. Meyer Kahn used to come here into this shop when he was at school. Now he runs South African Breweries. They used to come by and eat raw fish. He was a nice fellow. Yes, a nice fellow." Mr. Fong is silent for a moment. "I know a little Yiddish. I learned it from the Kahn family. This country," he says, "is *fershimmild*— finished."

Every day, at two o'clock, Jai stops whatever he is doing to listen to the BBC World Service. For some reason, the reception is clearer at two. He will excuse himself if he is talking to a customer; the BBC is inviolate. Jai looks at his watch and turns on the radio. The voice is crackly, indistinct, and he bends his head low to hear the announcer.

Jai trusts the BBC. He says it is the only reliable way to find out what is happening in his own country. Today, the lead item is about upheaval in Lebanon. Next is a report on American funding for the contras in Nicaragua.

The radio broadcast not only provides Jai with a window into his society, it offers a wider vista, making him feel a little more like a citizen of the world than a shopkeeper in Brits. Listening to the BBC is a ritual for those who feel isolated at home and disconnected from abroad.

The broadcast has a short item about Mrs. Thatcher, and then a final story on glasnost in the Soviet Union. Nothing about South Africa. We are no longer such a fashionable news story, Jai says.

He locks up the shop and gets into his Volkswagen. He wants to pop over to the CNA (Central News Agency) before going home for lunch. Jai doesn't bother locking the doors of the car; it's so battered, he can't imagine anyone stealing it. Crime is a problem, though. Over the last few years, Primindia has been beset by burglaries. The Bhulas themselves were robbed not very long ago. Two years before, some residents of Primindia decided to form a street patrol; Jai refers to it as a "vigilante" group. The men patrolled the neighborhood at night armed with clubs. Jai was asked to join but declined.

Jai drives up Kruis Street and crosses the railway line. The town police, he says, often stop cars at the crossing to randomly check indicator lights and registrations. The drivers are inevitably black. Often, the police stop taxis or kombis. "Perhaps they justify it," Jai says with a half-smile, "by saying that they are only trying to ensure the safety of the people in the taxis."

The Town Council has announced plans to build a pedestrian overpass to replace the Kruis Street railway crossing. Government policy, they say, deems all railway crossings dangerous and mandates their elimination wherever possible. Jai and many of the other Indian merchants see a different motive. The Town Council wants to restrict the flow of traffic into the Indian shopping area in order to help business in the white area. Many Indians see this as a tightening of the screw that started with the closing off of Tom Street as the principal entrance to Brits.

The policy is only natural, Jai says, noting that Brits has a new Conservative party MP who supports a return to traditional apartheid policies. The new MP, Mr. Andrew Gerber, a quiet, scholarly former predikant, believes the present Nationalist government is preparing to give power away to the blacks. Gerber rode a wave of dissatisfaction with the Nationalists. In Parliament, the Conservative Party replaced the liberal Progressive Federalist Party as the official opposition, and in the Transvaal, the CP trounced the Nationalists, taking the same share of the province's seats that the Nationalists had won from the United Party back in 1948.

In town, Jai drives by the book. He comes to a standstill at stop signs and looks both ways. He does not want anyone to have an excuse to pull him over. He parks the car directly across the street from the CNA and puts five cents in the meter. Twenty minutes.

Jai walks by Travolta's Take-Aways and notices a number of barefooted black women swathed in plaid woolen blankets. They are farm workers from Venda and KwaNdebele that the local farmers import from the homelands. Every couple of weeks, the farmer hauls them into town on the back of his truck to buy supplies. Normally, they are taken to Primindia, but some farmers bring them to the *kafees* in town. Jai suspects this is happening more and more.

Jai will not enter Travolta's Take-Aways. He remembers the owner once serving a white man ahead of him even though Jai was first. Jai put down what he was buying and walked out. Jai finds that the recent white immigrants to South Africa, the Greeks and Portuguese, are even more race-conscious than the Afrikaner. They are usually uneducated, he says, and their economic competition is the black man.

"Where there should be natural alliances," he says, "between poor whites and blacks—there are firmer divisions. That suits the government. You've got a divided working class. The white immigrants see black people as a threat. I can almost forgive the poor white who says the black man took his job away from him. What I can't understand are the educated people who think that way. It's always believed that prejudice comes from ignorance.

"The poor white is led to think the way he thinks. That Conservative party propaganda about taxes, about paying for black schools and then the kids burning them down—those rallying cries are directed toward the poor white. The whites always complain about taxes. That they are the minority paying for the majority," he says, and pauses. "But that is the price of power," he adds with a smile.

CNA is Brits's main stationery store. It is a national chain that sells newspapers, magazines, candy, and cards. Jai walks over to the magazine rack. He is looking for a publication called *New Socialist*, but it is not there. They sometimes carry it. He will buy a music magazine instead. He gets in line behind two women; an old lady waits behind him. He is the only non-white in the shop. Jai's manner here is icy. A young man and woman are working behind the register. When it is Jai's turn, he places the magazine on the counter. The girl smiles at him; Jai doesn't acknowledge it. He pays for the magazine, and the girl says, *"Dankie."* Jai, quite formal, replies, "Thank you," and walks out.

Jai finds that the white shopkeepers in town seem to run their stores for their own convenience rather than that of the customer. They seem annoyed when asked questions and regard a request as an imposition. In general, the proprietors seem to consider customers an occupational hazard of doing business.

If there is one thing that the normally fractious collection of Indian merchants can agree upon, it is that the Afrikaner does not have a head for business. The ineptitude of the Afrikaner businessman is a running joke in Primindia. The Afrikaner, they say, does not plan for the future. He does not ingratiate himself with his customers, treating them instead like interlopers. He behaves as if opening early and closing late is cheating.

The Indians shake their heads at Afrikaner business techniques: if there is a surplus of a product, they say, the Afrikaner will raise the price. If a product is regularly selling out, he will stop stocking it. Afrikaners don't seem to mind paying the price of business failure; bankruptcy in Brits is common and is often used as a means of preserving assets and starting fresh. There is little onus against bankruptcy among whites. In Primindia, bankruptcy is regarded as the depth of disgrace and is to be avoided at all cost.

In the white business community, Jai says, it was always considered nasty and low-class to sell to the black man. Beginning in the late 1950s, he says, the Afrikaner basically ceded the largest market in the country to the Indian. The white attitude was that the black man had little money to spend and what he did have he usually spent on beer. Let the Indian cater to them.

As a result, many Indians, particularly rural Indians, became wealthy by selling to the black man. Success put them in an awkward spot. Affluent Indians in Brits and elsewhere are both victims and beneficiaries of apartheid. They have profited from the white man's suppression of the black, but are deprived of the economic and political freedom of the white man. Their success has accentuated their dilemma; the more prosperous they are, the more subjugated they feel. They have the white man's burden, but not his freedom. Indian merchants in Brits seem to rail against apartheid mainly because it prevents them from living in the style that they can afford.

Jai does not pride himself on being a good businessman. He recoils at being thought "sharp." But after nine years in the shop, he knows a thing or two about retailing. He knows that he is busier at the beginning and end of every month, and to concentrate his sales at those times. And he also knows the essential reason why the white businessman in Brits is not more prosperous. "You cannot be prejudiced and be a good businessman," he says.

LIFE SPIES A PARKING PLACE in front of the post office. He has promised to mail a letter for someone in Oukasie. Life makes a U-turn on Murray Avenue to ensure that he gets there before anyone else. An empty place in front of the post office. It must be his lucky day.

He has already dropped off the following passengers: two fac-

tory workers at Verwoerd Avenue, named after Prime Minister
Hendrik Verwoerd, the intellectual architect of apartheid; a girl
who works in the kitchen at the Wimpy Bar; and a woman who
wanted to get out in front of the town library ("You can only step
in that place," Life says with a smile, "if you're bringing a cup of
tea for the *baas*").

As Life is maneuvering his car into the space, he grazes the
fender of a late-model American car in front of him. A white man
is sitting in the driver's seat. He turns slowly to see who it is and
when he does, performs a classic double take. He gets out of his car
and gives Life a lingering once-over and then walks to the rear of
his car to inspect the bumper. He wears the farmer's uniform:
khaki shirt, khaki shorts, khaki-colored knee socks, and black bro-
gans. He is a stout fellow with knees that seem the size of hubcaps.

Life's hand shakes slightly as he lights a Rothman. He stands
off to the side, not looking. It's bad luck to look. The farmer bends
over, examining the bumper minutely. Nothing. The farmer makes
one last inspection, hoping to find something. Not a scratch. He
glares at Life. Life nods. The farmer gets in the car and drives away.
Life smiles broadly, draws deeply on his cigarette, and says, "My
ancestors must be with me today."

Until last year, the post office had separate entrances for black and
white. In 1986, as part of its reform policy, the Nationalist government repealed the Reservation of Separate Amenities Act of 1953.
That act, the most conspicuous of social segregation laws, authorized separate buildings, services, and conveniences for white and
non-white. After the law was overturned, government buildings
were required to have one entrance for all. But the repeal affected
only public buildings, not private ones. Private amenities are under
the control of their owners or the local authorities. In Brits, only
the government buildings are now "open." All the restaurants in
town post RIGHT OF ADMISSION RESERVED signs, allowing them to
bar non-whites. Rest rooms at all the local filling stations still post
the distinctive signs for white and black: a black silhouette of a
man on a white background for whites, the reverse for blacks.

Life walks inside the post office, and drops some coins in the
stamp machine while a middle-aged white woman waits behind
him. As he is leaving, he says hello to one of the black street
sweepers outside of the post office. She is the sister of a friend of
his. The street sweepers wear bright orange dusters and use long

sharpened sticks to spear pieces of paper. Behind them, they drag a wheeled garbage can. Outside the post office the five public phones are monopolized by blacks. "The Boers have their telephones at home," Life says.

The atmosphere in town is not the same today as it was only a few years ago. "It feels different to walk in town now," Life says. "It's freer. Most shops had a separate entrance for blacks. If a Boer was walking toward you in those days, you had to jump out of the way. He'd say, 'Kaffir, can't you find a better place to walk?'

"There were no toilets in town for blacks. Not even at the taxi or bus ranks. I remember once they arrested me for passing water next to the taxi rank. That was seventy-eight, seventy-nine. Now there's a toilet at Sales House [a local store]. But it's far away and I've never been there."

There is an unspoken protocol between whites and blacks in town. A black man will never acknowledge a white man unless the white does so first. Blacks and whites pass each other as though they existed in separate dimensions. When Life is in town, he does his best to make himself invisible.

Until 1986, when the Abolition of Influx Control Act was passed, blacks were required to carry reference books which they had to produce on demand by any authorized official. The act made it an offense for Africans, except those with the requisite exemption or permission, to remain in a prescribed area for longer than seventy-two hours. Between 10 P.M. and 5 A.M., blacks in Brits had to carry a permit or be subject to arrest. According to the South African President's Council, between 1916 and 1981 a total of 17,120,000 arrests were made for pass law violations.

"They used sirens at night so that we had to be out of town," says Life. "Except the maids—they could stay at white people's houses. But the police would search the maids' rooms to see if they were hiding anyone. The Brits municipal police, and the Special Branch, used to look for people." The Special Branch are plainclothes police who deal with "security matters."

"One time, I remember it was early Saturday morning. I was on the night shift at Firestone. They picked me up because I didn't have my pass. I stayed in jail until we had to go to court on Monday. 'Do you plead guilty or not guilty?' they asked. If you pled not guilty, they said your case was postponed. If you pled guilty, you just paid a fine and left. No one wished to say 'not guilty' because it meant you had to stay another night.

."Every time you went to town you had to carry your pass. I was arrested three times for not having my pass. Once by Piet Ras!" he says animatedly and laughs.

Piet Ras was a legend in Oukasie. His name is pronounced like a kind of mantra and always as though it were one word: *Piet*ras, with the accent on the first syllable. Ras was the police officer responsible for the township. "People thought he used some kind of muti," Life says. *Muti* is witch doctor's medicine.

Ras would drive into Oukasie on his motorcycle, which had a sidecar for his black assistant officer, and round up people who were brewing beer. He would make them walk to the police station carrying the evidence—barrels of beer—on their heads.

Weekends were the busiest times. Ras routinely arrested people for pass violations. "If he found you in town after nine without a 'special' " [a signed pass from one's employer], Life recalls, "he would arrest you." Early Sunday morning, a throng of as many as two hundred blacks, most of whom had been arrested for pass violations, could be found marching up Murray Avenue to the police station with Piet Ras leading the way. Often they would sing "Nkosi Sikelel i-Afrika" ("God Bless Africa"), the soaring hymn that has become the anthem of the antiapartheid movement. "The sound," Life remembers, "was very beautiful."

Ras was an equal opportunity enforcer. He was fond of catching whites for violating the Immorality Act which forbade "any immoral or indecent act" between a white and an African, Indian, or Coloured. Ras's black sidekick was named Finchy, and he had an attractive girlfriend who used to visit him from Soweto. At the time, she needed a permit to do so. One day she went to see the Brits commissioner about a permit and he told her that she should meet him after work. She tipped off Finchy, and he and Piet Ras followed them. The commissioner picked her up in his car. Just before reaching his farm, he stopped and took her in the bushes. When the *delicto* was about to become *flagrante*, Finchy snapped a picture and Ras arrested the commissioner. Ras delighted in flashing the snapshots around town.

Today, Piet Ras is the town's coroner. Small and trim, with a pencil mustache and oiled black hair, he looks like a well-preserved silent film star. "Sometimes the job was easy," says Ras. "House break-ins. Never any bank robberies. No hard drugs. Only *dagga* [marijuana]. Mostly the blacks used it, but some whites went to buy it from them. They'd grow it on the farm, near the river. I hardly ever had to fight. Sometimes, if you see one in town and he's wobbling all over the road, you call out, 'Hey, uncle, you're drunk.' Then he takes out a knife and says, 'I'll fuck you up.' There were a few murders. Most of them black on black. On the weekends."

His job is quieter now. "I've worked in the mortuary for twenty years now. I go to the police station to check for bodies. Mostly old age, but there are many, many suicides among whites. They buy a bottle of rum, some Coke, and go to the Hartbeesport Dam, put the exhaust in the car, and drink and die. Blacks hang themselves. They take a piece of wire, attach it to a tree, then kick the chair away. Mostly on the farms. About sixty to seventy blacks kill themselves a year, and about one hundred whites."

Life has only one passenger left, and she wants to be dropped off at Kahn & Kahn's furniture store at the end of Murray Avenue. Life passes the town's police station on the left, a low-slung brick building whose windows are covered by horizontal slats which allow those inside to see out, but prevent those outside from seeing in. Across the street is the old Molani Hotel, which has a disco on Friday and Saturday nights. Right of Admission Reserved. He passes Travolta's Take-Aways on the right (the chips there, he says, are greasy), and the CNA, where Life bought his treasured copy of *Ebony*.

Life turns left at the end of Murray Avenue, and lets his last customer out at Kahn & Kahn. Meyer Kahn, the son of one of the founders, is the local boy who made good; he is chairman of South African Breweries. Kahn & Kahn concentrates on the black customer. Blacks generally buy on the installment plan. Like the other furniture stores in town, they sell everything in "suites." A burgundy-colored bedroom suite with two speakers embedded on either side of the mirrored headboard is displayed in the window. Price: R599. Monthly payment: R35.40.

Life parks the car. He wants to make a stop at the town's one *muti* store—A. D. M. Kruie—on Railway Street at the southern end of Murray Avenue. It's a tiny place, a closet arboretum. Behind the counter, plant bulbs with luminous tentacles float in jars of murky water. Long, fantastically shaped roots dangle from the ceiling. Life is startled to find a young Afrikaner fellow working in the shop. But Life recognizes him as the owner's son who has been learning about *muti* since he was a small boy.

Life asks for some *sekanama* root. B & B's Kidney and Bladder
Mixture just hasn't done the trick. The boy retreats to the back
room and returns with a large, round, pink bulb with a tangle of
stringy roots. Life explains how it works: the bulb is placed in
boiling water for several minutes and then you drink the water as
hot as you can stand it. "It soothes the stomach," he says, "and
helps the digestion." Life points out an onion-shaped root called
mathubafala, which has the same properties. Next to it is some
letsoka, a root used by the Shangaan tribe and occasionally by local
witch doctors to color their hair red.

Muti is routinely used by most everyone in Oukasie. Only as a
last resort do people consult a doctor, and the one they go to is Dr.
Pieter Miskin, a slow-moving, plain-spoken man who has a clinic
around the block from A. D. M. Kruie. Miskin is one of two white
physicians in town who have black practices. "Even businessmen
and teachers use muti," Miskin says, "and they will have marks on
them from witch doctors. For ulcers, I've seen little cuts over the
area of complaint. Muti has a lot of medicinal properties that some
of our medicine has. I had a fellow come in who had eczema on his
hands. I treated him with cortisone, and it improved a little. He
went to a witch doctor, though, who cured him completely."

Blacks, he says, suffer from the same diseases as whites, with
a few exceptions. They have more venereal diseases, particularly
gonorrhea. Ulcers and tuberculosis afflict more blacks than whites.
The men get gastritis and dyspepsia from drinking; after a week-
end, he says, some of them are "polluted" with alcohol. "In general,
they have very little practical knowledge about health," he says.
"For example, when their children have a high fever, they bundle
them up and the heat can't escape.

"But I've discovered some things that are very remarkable.
Their degree of self-control and self-discipline is extraordinary.
Men can be in great pain and will not show it. With children of five
or six, I sometimes notice in the urine that they have ketones
which indicates a breakdown in protein, perhaps from hunger. I ask
them when they last ate. It might be three or four in the afternoon,
and they haven't eaten that day. They don't complain. If you give
them a painful injection, they don't show it. They won't cry."

Life counts out the change for the Sekanama root. He appreciates
the convenience of the B & B's Mixture, but he does not completely
trust white man's medicine. He doesn't entirely trust *muti* either,

but his attitude is that it can't hurt to try both. He will have his
sister make up the *muti* for him when he gets home. He smiles at
the young fellow as he walks out. "He knows his *muti*," Life says
admiringly.

IT WAS THE COMING OF THE RAILROAD that literally put
Brits on the map. In 1906, a siding was constructed along the Pretoria to Rustenburg line at what is now the grain co-op on Tom
Street. The siding made the middle of nowhere into a place—a
station. And where the trains stopped, a gallimaufry of Jewish and
Indian traders suddenly appeared to peddle goods to anyone who
happened to be there.

The railway divided the farm of Johan Nicholaas Brits in two.
He was not particularly pleased by this, but there was nothing he
could do about it. Louis Karovsky, a Jewish businessman married
to an Afrikaans woman, saw possibilities in the area and bought a
parcel of land north of the railway from farmer Brits. Karovsky
hired a surveyor to cut 940 half-acre plots for development and lay
out a system of streets. He allocated land for a police station, a fire
house, and each religious denomination (including space for a synagogue). He sketched out Murray Avenue as a thoroughfare wide
enough for farmers to turn their ox wagons around.

Brits was officially proclaimed a town in October of 1923. In a
brochure promoting the town, Karovsky called Brits a "gilt-edged
investment" and likened it to the south of France as a place "sooth-
ing and beneficial to the jaded bodies and nerves of working City
Dwellers." The brochure touts the advantages of citrus farming,
and the potential for growing tobacco "since the natives as well as
the rural population have taken to smoking cigarettes." A warning
at the bottom of the brochure states: NO COOLIES OR OTHER COL-
OURED PERSONS PERMITTED TO RESIDE OR OWN PROPERTY WITHIN
THE TOWN.

Within fifteen years, Brits was a small, rugged *plakkie-dorp*
(Afrikaans for a tin shantytown). Petrol was brought by donkey
train from Pretoria in forty-four-gallon drums. Babies were deliv-
ered at home by the local surgeon who doubled as the town under-

taker. The postman came once a week by horse and buggy and blew
a bugle when he arrived. At the local stores, women sat down to
tea on the front porch while their black servants did the shopping.

The women wore long dresses. The men wore *veldskoene*,
homemade shoes of soft leather. When the farmers went calling,
they rode bicycles to the young ladies' houses and carried their
white gabardine trousers in a satchel so they wouldn't get soiled.
Every girl had to learn to play a musical instrument and recitals
were given to prove it. For entertainment, boys would loiter about
the depot and watch the trains come in. People used to say that if
you wanted a grand funeral, you should die in Brits because everybody in town would come.

The old Union Hotel offered room and board for nine pounds
and ten shillings a month. Nearby, the police station boasted its
own blacksmith, Mr. Lions, who shod the horses of the four white
constables. The Bioscope stood across the street, where Kahn &
Kahn is now. It was a wooden structure with a zinc roof and everyone in town had his own seat. When it rained, water drilled the
roof and drowned out the dialogue. During the interval, when the
reels were being changed, the men would nip across the street to
the Brits Hotel for a shot of whiskey. The churches vainly coun-
seled their parishioners to swear off the sinful cinema. The townspeople loved American Westerns and Tarzan movies.

Mrs. Moss ran the Brits Hotel. She was a stout, gruff woman
who dressed in overalls and diamond earrings. Every morning at
ten, she settled in on the front stoop of the hotel with her two
black-and white Scottish terriers. She spent the morning gossiping
and smoking. Every night, fights broke out in the hotel. Sometimes
the farmers used bicycle chains. The bar had a swinging door and
Mrs. Moss would occasionally bounce customers herself. The hotel
sold Chandler's Beer, "the Beer of South Africa," the invention of
an Englishman who came to the Transvaal after forsaking the diamond trade. He said that he could make more from man's thirst
than his greed.

Tobacco was king in Brits. By the mid-1930s, Brits was the
largest tobacco-producing area in South Africa. Tobacco is a labor-
intensive crop and farmers used an average of two black workers
per hectare. Even today, tobacco seedlings are planted by hand.
Brits tobacco was unusual because it was grown in black turf,
rather than sandy soil, which made the leaf richer and more fragrant.

The biggest day of the year in Brits was always *Agterskot:* the day that tobacco farmers were paid by the cooperative. Farmers and their families rolled into town on donkey carts. Murray Avenue was brimming with people. The hotel bars could hardly pour the liquor fast enough. The farmers sauntered around town with great rolls of bills; they liked to feel the notes in their hands. Secondhand car dealers arrived from Pretoria and the local garages lined up all their cars, new and used. Farmers would pay cash for a motorcar and leave their cart in the dust. Sometimes the farmer didn't know how to drive, and the car would sputter off, halting and backfiring.

Election Day was the second biggest day of the year. Before the voting, the United party and the Nationalist party would hold rallies. Speakers were jeered; fisticuffs were frequent. Brits was virulently anti-British. In 1943, three parties were competing for the seat from Brits: the United party, whose moderate candidate was the current Member of Parliament; the deeply conservative, pro-Nazi Ossewabrandwag which had come into being after the 1938 commemoration of the Great Trek; and the upstart Nationalist party, which was the party of Hendrik Verwoerd, apartheid, and anti-imperialism.

J. E. Potgieter was the Nationalist party candidate. Slight and scholarly, but a fiery speaker, Potgieter had been taught by Verwoerd at the University of Stellenbosch and had originally intended to be a minister. Potgieter defeated the incumbent United party candidate by two thousand votes and held the seat until his retirement in 1977. Brits's voting presaged the coming dominance of the Nationalist party, for in 1948 the Nationalists captured a parliamentary majority which they have never relinquished.

During the years leading up to World War II, Brits's sympathies were with Germany. "It was a rough time here before the war," says the elder Dr. Friedland, who first came to Brits in 1937. "It was unpleasant for us. The people at the Union Hotel where we stayed were so anti-British they were pro-Nazi. They said 'Heil Hitler' at dinner. During the war, they hardly even bothered to teach English; they would just let the kids go out and play during the English period."

From the early 1950s through the late 1960s, Brits remained a poky farming town. The most vexing problem—more of an annoyance, really, than a problem—was the black location. The Old Location, as it was known, was a necessary source of commercial and domestic labor, but it was simply too close. The Town Council wanted to move it, but the question was where.

The issue of the location became more important when Brits was selected as a Border Industry area by the central government in 1969. The government's policy was to get industry to move away from the PWV Triangle (Pretoria, Witwatersrand, Vaal) to the rural areas near the homelands. Black workers from the homelands would then have a short commute to white South Africa, and would not have to move to the cities. The government offered tax abatements and wage subsidies to companies that moved to Border Industry areas.

The policy was a legacy of grand apartheid and the latest wrinkle in the homelands policy. The homelands policy stated that all blacks were citizens of one of ten black homelands created by the government and were "temporary sojourners" in South Africa, where they went to sell their labor. While blacks comprised 73 percent of the population of South Africa, the homelands constituted only 13 percent of the land—and not very good land at that. Blacks became so-called new foreigners when the South African parliament conferred "independence" on their putative homelands. The "new foreigner" was prohibited by section 10 of the Urban Areas Act from remaining in an urban area for longer than seventy-two hours without permission from the authorities. The goal of the policy was succinctly stated in 1977 by the minister of Bantu affairs and development, Dr. Connie Mulder: "No more black South Africans."

Under the border industry policy, factories flocked to Brits. The new Brits industrial area would enormously increase the job market for local blacks. But the Town Council did not want the location to expand to accommodate those workers. The majority of the new workers would be coming from Bophuthatswana. With thousands of blacks commuting to Brits every day, the prospect was inescapable that Oukasie would swell in size.

At the same time, the town wanted to provide for the influx of white managers and the Council set aside a new extension next door to the black township. It was called Elandsrand and had space for several hundred homes. There was no way around it: another place for the location had to be found.

In 1969, the government, at the Town Council's urging, built two thousand homes in a black township called Mothutlung, twenty kilometers northeast of Brits on the border of Bophuthat-swana. The original plan, in line with the homelands policy, was for the people of the location to move to Mothutlung and then for Mothutlung to be incorporated into Bophuthatswana. But the plan went awry when His Excellency, Dr. Lucas M. Mangope, the president of Bophuthatswana, saw that non-Tswanas were moving into Mothutlung. Bophuthatswana, he maintained, was a Tswana country and he did not want it polluted by other tribes. Construction was halted and people stopped moving. Only then did he incorporate it into Bophuthatswana.

After the debacle at Mothutlung, the Town Council did not want to make another mistake. It put one of the newer council members, the representative for Onderdorp, Dr. Ronald de la Rey, in charge of finding a place to move the people of the Old Location.

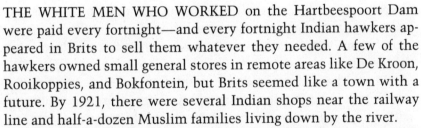

THE WHITE MEN WHO WORKED on the Hartbeespoort Dam were paid every fortnight—and every fortnight Indian hawkers appeared in Brits to sell them whatever they needed. A few of the hawkers owned small general stores in remote areas like De Kroon, Rooikoppies, and Bokfontein, but Brits seemed like a town with a future. By 1921, there were several Indian shops near the railway line and half-a-dozen Muslim families living down by the river.

The coolies—as Indians were called by the whites—were tolerated by the locals because they served a purpose. They dealt with the black man and the poor white, and were subservient enough to the white townspeople not to offend anyone. Whereas urban Indians were the subject of intense animosity and periodic campaigns to "send them back," the rural Indian was mostly left alone.

In the Transvaal, Indians were restricted from owning property, and their freedom of movement was curtailed by the Immigration Regulation Act of 1908 which required all Indians to carry passes. But Indian lawyers had discovered loopholes in the law that permitted merchants to establish businesses. The Indians in Brits were more concerned with commerce than with that upstart Mohandas Gandhi. Gandhi, a young lawyer who had arrived in South

Africa in 1893, was then evolving his technique of *satyagraha,*
which consisted of peaceful resistance to the government's restrictions on Indian residential and trading rights.

The Brits Indian community grew slowly. A simple zinc
mosque was built in 1924, at which time there were about sixty
Indians in town. Most of the men still had families in India. One
by one, wives and children were brought over when there was
money to do so. In 1938, a one-room brick schoolhouse on Tom
Street was opened for Indian children. There were twenty pupils
and one teacher, an Afrikaner. When the school needed to be expanded, money was raised by charging five cents a person to see
showings of Indian and American movies.

In the 1930s, Tom Street was a dusty, bustling thoroughfare teem-
ing with ox wagons, cars, and people of all colors. Dozens of shops
huddled next to each other and jutted out at odd angles. The shopkeepers were a varied lot: most were Indian, but there were a handful of Jews, a few Afrikaners, and two black shoemakers.

Every two weeks, local farmers would bring their workers to
town to stock up on supplies. The farmers arrived in trucks or ox
wagons and off-loaded their laborers in the middle of the street.
Everything the workers could want or need was on Tom Street. If
any of them wandered across the railway line to the white shops,
they would be shooed away.

Primindia had one place of entertainment: the Paradise Cinema. It was not a theater, but an old two-story warehouse equipped
with a makeshift screen that showed mostly Indian movies, and
some American. Cardboard egg cartons lined the walls because
they were thought to help the acoustics.

After the Nationalists came to power in 1948, one of the first pieces
of legislation introduced by the government was the Group Areas
Act of 1950, mandating the residential segregation of all racial
groups. In introducing the bill, Dr. T. E. Dönges, minister of the
interior, said the measure was designed to ensure "the para-
mountcy of the white man and of Western civilization in South
Africa . . . in the interests of the material, cultural and spiritual
development of all races."

In many ways, the Group Areas Act had greater impact on
Indians than blacks. Control over the movement and residence of
blacks was traditionally accomplished through the pass laws and

the Urban Areas Act which prevented them from living near white residential areas. By the 1940s, however, Indians were not required to carry passes, and though they were restricted from particular residential areas by existing laws, they were often living in town centers next to or above their shops. Under the new bill, land was now set aside for Indians, as well as blacks and Coloured.

Brits's MP, J. E. Potgieter, had petitioned the government *not* to move the town's Indian area. Brits's Indian area was in a unique position. Almost entirely Indian, it was already separated from white residential areas. The government agreed that it would be too difficult and too expensive to relocate the Indian population. So, in 1952, Primindia not only became the first Group Areas town in the Transvaal, but the only one that did not have to move. Named Primindia Township, it was proclaimed an Indian Exempted Area where only Indians could live and trade. The government allocated land for three streets and also established an Indian Management Committee which reported to the white Town Council.

The railroad was the dividing line. Everything south of it was reserved for Indians, everything north was whites only. The handful of blacks and Coloured who lived in Primindia were forced to move. Whites who owned land there had to sell and were not at all happy about it. The ruling also concentrated land ownership in Primindia into the hands of the existing Indian property owners. They were the only ones who could afford to buy the land that the whites had to sell.

Elsewhere in the Transvaal, the act functioned as intended and had precisely the opposite result that it did in Brits. Most local authorities successfully agitated for the removal of Indian shops and residences from the central business areas to at least a mile out of town.

In 1960, the English-born South African actor and director Jamie Uys was preparing to make a movie called *The Hellions*, about a gang of turn-of-the-century outlaws who menace a small town. All was ready except that Uys needed a location that looked like a Wild West American town. When the production scout brought Uys to Brits, the director found what he wanted. Primindia was perfect. To Uys, it looked exactly the way he imagined an American town of the 1890s.

Uys filmed *The Hellions* on Tom Street in three weeks. The

movie featured a cast of mostly British character actors, and was
eventually released in America by Columbia Pictures. Out of grat-
itude to the people of Primindia for allowing him to use Tom
Street, Uys offered to pave it. He donated about half of what was
necessary to do so. But Tom Street stayed dusty for another decade,
until the white Town Council came up with the other half of the
money.

By the early 1970s, the population of Primindia had increased
tenfold since the 1930s, while the geographic area remained the
same size. Families were squeezed into tiny flats and houses, and
people regularly complained to the Indian Management Committee to do something. But the committee was part of the problem.

The committee members were all Indian landlords, and any
expansion of Primindia would undermine the monopoly they had
on the township's land. They could charge tenants whatever they
wanted, and the tenant had no choice but to pay.

Several rebel committees were formed in Primindia to press
for more land and for an end to the domination of the landlords.
These committees petitioned the central government and eventually got results. In 1972, the government provided a land extension to Primindia and constructed thirty-three council houses.

But the council houses were allocated to friends and family of
the landlords; those with neither wealth nor influence were shut
out. In 1981, the tenants of several old houses behind the shop Shoe
Parade on Tom Street were given 500 percent increases in rent.
When the tenants proved unable to pay, the landlords served them
with eviction notices and threatened to demolish the houses. Some
of the tenants had lived there for fifty years. A meeting was called
and a group called the Ten House Committee was formed to fight
the landlords.

Jaiprakash Bhula attended that meeting and joined the committee, which ultimately helped preserve the houses. When the
crisis was averted, a more permanent committee was formed to
fight for more land and Jaiprakash Bhula was elected chairman
of it.

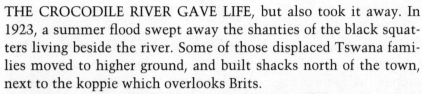

THE CROCODILE RIVER GAVE LIFE, but also took it away. In 1923, a summer flood swept away the shanties of the black squatters living beside the river. Some of those displaced Tswana families moved to higher ground, and built shacks north of the town, next to the koppie which overlooks Brits.

White towns all across the Transvaal had locations at their edges, black satellite communities that provided labor for farms and stores. In 1905, the Lagden Commission had advanced the idea of territorial separation of black and white and approved the establishment of segregated "locations" for urban blacks. The Natives Land Act of 1913, the Native Affairs Act of 1920, and the Natives (Urban Areas) Act of 1923 codified the principles of segregated locations and institutionalized the administration, financing, and policing of African locations.

In 1928, Brits Old Location was formally "established" by the government as a black residential area on land owned and administered by the local white municipality. In the early 1930s, the government built approximately two hundred simple corrugated iron shacks in the Old Location, many of which are still standing.

Oukasie grew. People started building places farther up toward the koppie. An area was named Greenside because it was so lush. The area around the entrance of Oukasie was known as Municipal, because the buildings there had been built by the municipality. Municipal had a general store, a *kafee* which served cold drinks, and a tiny bakery. The poorest area was called Masenkeng, Tswana for "shacks." There were only three water taps in the whole township and no toilets.

Some of the more enterprising men hired carts to haul coal and wood from the train station and sell them in the township. Most of the residents of the location worked on nearby farms, and every morning, farmers pulled up in trucks or wagons to pick up their workers. Everyone piled in back. The farmer and his dog rode in front. Those who worked in town walked. A bicycle was the sign of a wealthy man; the Mercedes of Oukasie.

As the Indian area expanded, more blacks started working in

the shops and warehouses of Primindia. The blacks regarded the Indians as *baases*—which the Indians usually insisted on being called—and sometimes wryly referred to them as "black Afrikaners."

During the 1940s, Oukasie was considered a smart address. Parties were frequent. Someone would get a gramophone and some Gumba-Gumbas, as amplifiers were called. The music was jazz. Township dandies wore double-breasted suits and hats with curled-up brims known as "Buttersbies." The stylish ladies wore taffeta dresses, half-moon hats with veils, and "Manyattas," shoes with thick soles made from car tires.

Blacks were barred from buying liquor and beer was home-brewed out of maize or black corn. People also drank *mampoer*, a strong alcoholic drink made from the plumlike fruit of the marula tree. Some smoked *dagga*. There were tamer forms of entertainment, as well, such as church concerts, soccer games, and occasional boxing matches.

In the 1950s, the white municipality began issuing permits for blacks to live in the township. They were charged five shillings and six pence a month for their stands—"five and six," as it was called —and the land was allocated by the superintendent. The permits made some people feel more secure, but the older residents of the township say they always knew that Oukasie was temporary. No black residential area in South Africa was ever considered permanent. Over the years, rumors would spread through the township that they were moving, but then nothing happened. No one seemed too worried. The people of Oukasie were permanently temporary.

Only when the government built Mothutlung in 1969 did the threat seem imminent. A few people moved there, but most were afraid that the town would be incorporated into Bophuthatswana, which would result in their automatically losing their South African citizenship.

Life remembers first hearing about Lethlabile in 1983. He had just quit Firestone and was running his shebeen. "In 1983, people were told that they should not build new houses in the township because they were going to be moved. But by 1984," Life says, "people saw no sign of removal and began building again."

In June of 1985, Life recalls, the community councillors told a few people that they would be able to buy their own places in

Lethlabile. The councillors were traditionally seen as those blacks who were coziest with the white authorities. Most of them were shopkeepers who were elected in a sham vote in which only a handful of people in the community participated.

On December 7, 1985, the councillors held their first and last meeting. At the Catholic hall they announced that the people of Oukasie had to move to Lethlabile by the end of the year. They outlined how residents would be reimbursed for their houses and discussed the subsidies the government was offering. They said the government had promised that Lethlabile would not be incorporated into Bophuthatswana. The community was stunned, frightened, confused.

The following day a public meeting was organized, attended by more than eight hundred people. The residents of the township elected a committee of eight to represent them and lead the resistance to what the government was calling a "voluntary" removal. All eight men elected were union activists. The committee was named the Brits Action Committee (BAC) and its chairman was Mr. Marshall Buys.

AFTERNOON

LIFE IS FLOATING. No passengers, no destination, no place he has to be. He can return to Oukasie or head over to the taxi rank in Primindia or the Thari bus terminal. It's lunchtime and Life figures there may be some customers in Primindia.

He crosses the railway line and drives down Kruiṣ Street, passing Bhula Prema and Sons on the left, where he bought a pair of shoes last year that have held up pretty well. Life washes his shoes once a week with soap and water.

He turns left on Tom Street and pulls into the taxi rank, which is just at the top of Carel Street, across from Hegel's. The taxi rank here mainly serves workers from the industrial area who have walked over to do some shopping in Primindia.

The area is littered with beer cans and newspapers, and four or five taxis are already parked there. The drivers are standing around, talking and smoking. Life sees Sello, who is waiting for a ride.

"Ah, Life," Sello says, "you are a member of the working classes today." Life smiles.

Sello is on his way back to Firestone, where he is the union's highest ranking shop steward. He is also, along with Life, one of the original members of the Brits Action Committee. Sello has a very high forehead and very small ears and talks in a rapid staccato. He always seems a step or two ahead of everyone else. If you ask him what he thinks about something, he invariably replies, "I don't *think*, I'm involved."

Sello needs a ride to the industrial area and hops into Life's taxi. Life drives down Carel Street, passing the Edward's store going up and the plots for the Indian extension, and then crosses the Pretoria Road on his way to the Thari terminal. Life makes his way through the terminal and enters the industrial area.

The industrial area is a flat sprawl of drab factories and two-story offices. All the buildings look similar and it is easy to get lost.

Ten thousand people work in the industrial area, nearly 60 percent of whom are black. The black factory worker's income comes to about R800 a month, compared to an average of about R400 for a nonfactory worker in Oukasie. In 1984, eighty-three factories and companies were operating here. But in the last five years, some 20 percent have closed or gone out of business. Most have attributed the downturn to the combination of sanctions, a weak economy, and strong unions. Alfa Romeo closed its factory in 1983. Femco did the same two years ago and Steelbrite, which makes steel furniture, closed last year and then reopened in Bophuthatswana, where unions are illegal and wages lower. Just last week, a coffin manufacturer employing about eighty workers announced that it was shutting its doors, firing its workers, and moving to Bophuthatswana.

The early shift is over. Hundreds of workers are sitting outside the factories eating bread and drinking Coke. There are no trees, no cover of any kind, no benches or places to sit. Many of the women crouch down in the dirt, shrouding their heads with dark green garbage bags for protection against the afternoon sun. The light is clear and dazzlingly bright and the sky is high and vast.

Life drives into the imposing entrance of Firestone. The factory is divided into segments, each of which is painted a different shade of green, causing the plant to resemble the carapace of a colossal insect. The plant, built in 1971–72 on what had been a tobacco field, is the most modern tire factory in South Africa. Firestone has about seven hundred employees, five hundred of whom are black. Inside the cavernous plant, raw rubber is vulcanized with stearic acid, pounded into long thin swatches, stabilized with steel, fitted into a mold, cured, and then baked in huge ovens which, twenty minutes later, spit out the steel-belted tires, hot and smoking, like enormous cookies on a tray.

Life parks the taxi, and he and Sello walk over to a circle of men who are talking in front of the factory. They are union leaders, and Life knows most of them. The men question Sello about an upcoming meeting with management concerning an artisan program in the factory. The union is unhappy that Firestone is not allocating more places for black workers. Sello tells them that he will be demanding a guaranteed number. As a shop steward, Sello's principal responsibility seems to be listening to workers' complaints. He has no hours, no office, no work station, but he is a powerful figure at the factory.

Life is nostalgic about Firestone. He talks about it like a proud alumnus recalling his days at his alma mater. "I worked at Firestone for seven years," Life says. "I never worked a full week though. I would work a lot of overtime. I enjoyed my job. I was proud that they assigned me important work. The boss was always giving me difficult jobs to do. I was a hard worker.

"My boss was not too bad. Sometimes you actually find some white guys who are color-blind. If he's a hard worker, he just wants the job to be done. He doesn't care about your color. You know, the Afrikaner likes talking about fishing and hunting. He doesn't really like to work. They love to talk about their farms when they are at the factory. Sometimes they sit, squatting like this"—he demonstrates, bending down on his haunches—"having their cigarettes, for one and a half hours. I can't even stay like that for ten minutes. I don't know how they do it.

"There was one manager who used to shoo them away. 'If you want to talk about your farms,' he would say, 'go back there.' He was a very hard worker. The inside of his hand was so rough—rougher than the bottoms of my feet. He would come over, and if you weren't doing your job, he would put his hand on the back of your neck and say, *Come on, man*. He could hold cured tires in his hands. They were over a hundred degrees [Celsius]. Whew!

"Then a new white man, replacing my old boss, was hired. The new guy wanted to fuck me around. He didn't know what he was doing, and he would order me to do things that I knew were wrong. I only defied his orders when I thought it was right to do so. Things never got back to normal.

"The head manager called us together, and then decided to shift me to another department. It involved running some sophisticated machinery, and I was given more responsibility and an office. I had to do complicated mathematics, calculating sigma values and all that.

"I told the manager that things were worse now: he hadn't relieved me of any responsibility, and I'm not getting paid any more. I was also a shop steward at the time. It was too much responsibility for too little money. I told him I did not want to sit at a desk and wear a tie every day. All I wanted was a good reward for the work that I was doing. It's quite good to have responsibility; it makes you want to live. But you have to be rewarded."

Life and Sello were present at the creation of the unions in Brits. In 1977, an organization called the Young Christian Workers (YCW) began recruiting members in Oukasie. Life, Sello, David Modimoeng, and Jacob Moatse joined up. At the time there were no black trade unions in Brits and the WCW was exploring the possibility of unionizing the factories. In 1979, the government passed the Labor Relations Act which established the right of black workers to form independent trade unions.

The first union in Brits was organized that same year by David Mdimoeng at Femco, an auto parts manufacturer. A year later, Sello, Life, and a handful of others formed a union steering committee at Firestone. All the members of that committee but one were from Oukasie.

The steering committee held a sign-up for workers who wanted to join the union. Under the law, Firestone was required to recognize the union when at least half the workers signed up. About 70 percent of the workers did, though when questioned by management, that number dropped to about 60 percent. "They questioned each and every worker," Life says. "The workers were scared. A lot of people told management that someone else had signed up, not them."

Management initially refused to negotiate with the steering committee, but then relented. Local management had little experience in dealing with a union. "In Brits," says Life, "the unionization of Firestone was the only company where recruitment was short and simple. I couldn't believe it when they said it was okay. I didn't think they were stupid, but I thought they might be playing tricks on us. It wasn't the company that was sincere, it was the plant manager."

The recognition agreement was signed in 1983 and merely stated that management recognized the right of the union to negotiate on behalf of all the workers. It also outlined the activities and the election procedures of the shop stewards. When the elections for shop stewards were held, both Life and Sello won handily.

The union has struck Firestone a number of times since 1983. For the most part, Firestone has taken a hard line. The company believed that because it had been fair early in the process, it could be tough later. Sello admits that the strikes have often been sty-mied. "We have had to settle for face-saving agreements," he says.

But the unions are now a fact of life for management; they must consult with them on everything from the machines on the shop floor to the hamburgers in the cafeteria. "The company has a problem," says Sello. "It looks like workers, not the management, are in control."

The unions are not exactly drunk with power, but they are a bit tipsy. They have a certain amount of leverage and they use the leverage they have. They don't hold it in reserve. Life is more con-servative; he thinks using the power diminishes it.

The union considers Oukasie as much of an issue as worker safety. In Oukasie, unionists became the leaders of the fight against the removal, while the fight became part of the union's agenda with the company. Management complained that they were forced to spend more time discussing Oukasie than problems in the factory. They accused the shop stewards of "politicizing" the collective bargaining process.

But the shop stewards saw no division between the commu-nity and the factory. "The unions," says Life, "have never limited themselves to direct bargaining; they were always part of the strug-gle as a whole. We didn't have political organizations in Oukasie. The unions had to do something. If it were not for the concern of the unions, we already might have been dragged away."

Firestone initially saw the removal to Lethlabile as a way of undercutting the power of the unions: when workers had houses and mortgages and lived farther from the factory, they would not be so concerned about union issues. Firestone, like most of the factories, offered a variety of incentives for their workers to move to Lethlabile. "At one point," says Sello, "one white guy in indus-trial relations spent all his time trying to get people to move."

But Firestone was on to something. Life witnessed their strat-egy working. "I saw people," he says, "who were strong turn weak because of those housing loans. They want to enslave people by the things they give them."

In 1981, Federale Volksbeleggings, a South African conglomerate, bought 75 percent of Firestone (South Africa) from the parent com-pany Firestone Tire & Rubber in the United States. The agreements specified that Federale would have access to technological information from any Firestone facility worldwide. In 1987, Federale bought out the remaining 25 percent.

Sean Wustman is one of the new breed of young Afrikaner managers Federale brought in. His responsibility is dealing with the unions. "Most of the companies around here think we give too much to the unions," he says. "We've heard workers say that they run the plant. If it makes them feel good to say that they are running the place, let them say it. They could cripple the plant if they wanted. But what would happen? Seven hundred people would lose their jobs.

"The white conservatives in Brits can't accept the fact that you must talk to your work force. On the farms, if the worker doesn't do something, you get rid of him. We strive not to be in a win-lose situation here. We strive for a win-win situation. Over the past few years, we've had only about ten dismissals. It was just a few years ago that if a chap wasn't doing a good job, you'd take him in the back and give him a good clump."

Wustman thinks that the union sometimes uses its power capriciously. Last week, he says, the plant came to a halt over some french fries. Lunch was fish and chips, but there were no chips because the deep-fryer had broken. The kitchen made pap. The workers complained that you could not eat fish with pap. The kitchen made frozen steaks, but the workers wanted fish and held a work stoppage for three hours.

Firestone was a signatory to the Sullivan Principles, the 1977 code drafted by the Reverend Leon Sullivan, which called for U.S. companies in South Africa to desegregate facilities, pay equal wages for equal work, and improve job training and advancement. By 1986, most U.S. companies in South Africa were complying. Wustman says that even though the company is now South African and not American, the racial policies will not move backward. "Federale has a code just as strict," he says. The much-vaunted Sullivan Principles, he says, were mainly window dressing anyway. "I was one of those who had to do the report every year," he says. "Sullivan mainly entailed a reporting function. You can make a company look very good on paper. Many companies had black supervisors doing things on paper that they were not doing on the shop floor." Few if any American-owned companies in South Africa had a single white employee supervised by a black one.

Wustman says his job would be much easier if it weren't for Oukasie. When he sits down to negotiate with the union over benefits, for example, he says they will bring up Oukasie. "They inject politics into everything," he says. But he concedes that Firestone misstepped on the Oukasie issue: early on, they donated R30,000 to build a nursery school in Lethlabile. "We were crucified on that by the unions," Wustman says.

"Oukasie is seen by the whites in Brits as a rat's nest. Because of Oukasie and Brits's bad reputation for labor, companies say they want to move here like a hole in the head. Bophuthatswana is only ten kilometers away. Our company position is that we don't support a forced removal. Our directors have contacted the government many times and told them that we have a problem here. We think something can be done to improve the place. We did a survey. Our highest absenteeism rate comes from Oukasie and they are the closest to the factory. I tell them, you should get rid of the bad elements and just keep the people who really want to stay and then get it upgraded."

The impromptu meeting breaks up and Sello and the others head inside. Life misses the paycheck at Firestone, but not the hours and the responsibility. He waves good-bye. The union men treat him with exaggerated courtesy, the way active soldiers behave toward pensioned-off veterans.

Life is getting hungry, and wants to get back to Oukasie. Sello asks Life if he will be at Playboy's later. Life smiles, as if to say, Where else shall I be?

●

TACKED TO THE WALL of de la Rey's study is a calendar (two years out of date); a yellowing photograph of The Department of Prisons' Commander and Staff, Brits, 1966, showing six seated white men in black hats and five standing black men in white hats (the stern-faced commander in the center is de la Rey's father); a snapshot from his daughter's wedding, in which a pretty, serious-faced young woman is wearing a white Victorian-style wedding dress; a yearbook photo of Yelena at university, her hair in a pert fifties flip; and a photograph of de la Rey in academic subfusc staring suspiciously at the camera, as though he were a member of one of those probably apocryphal tribes who believe the camera steals their souls.

A large home-entertainment unit with a color TV and stereo system presides over the living room. Next to it are shelves of bric-a-brac and books: *Practical Animal Husbandry, Birdlife in South Africa, Canine Surgery, Atlas of Dermatology, The Encyclopedia Brittanica,* and a biography of Hendrik Verwoerd.

De la Rey has had a shave before lunch. "Must do it for the public," he says. He is having boerewors, a spicy beef and pork sausage, roast potatoes, a green salad, brown bread (which he prefers to white), and coffee. The de la Reys, like most white families in town, have meat at virtually every meal. The meat, whether it is steak, lamb, or pork, is always well done. Yelena does most of the cooking even though she has black help in the house. The family eats in a small room off the kitchen, which is kept in shadow. No point in turning on the lights when it is so hot. The de la Reys do not have air-conditioning; only the public buildings in town do.

Morné is still in his pajama bottoms. He has on a T-shirt that shows a man on a surfboard hanging ten with the legend, FIRST IN THE SURF. He is finishing off his third ice-filled glass of Coke. Morné estimates that he drinks a liter of the stuff a day, and Yelena stocks up on the mega two-liter containers from Checkers in town.

"You'll never win the car at this rate," de la Rey tells Morné.

"I'll win it," Morné says.

Morné is preparing to take his matric exam, which is the week-long series of tests white South African students must pass to graduate from high school. De la Rey has promised him a new car if he gets five A's on his exams. If he does not, he will still get a car, only it will be a used one. Morné is confident that he will be driving a shiny new automobile at the University of Pretoria this February. De la Rey thinks Morné does not work hard enough, but he can't complain because Morné gets all A's anyway.

The phone rings. Morné leaps up from the table, grabs a piece of toast, and then dashes out of the kitchen, hurdling a sofa in the living room to get the phone before it rings a second time. De la Rey shakes his head at this and smiles. He is indulgent of Morné. He treats his son as though he were a prized calf with matchless bloodlines.

Morné retires to the patio, reclining on a chaise longue, munching on the cold toast. His exams begin in three days. The patio has a terra-cotta tile floor and a blue-and-orange-striped awning. Amidst the wicker chairs is a Ping-Pong table. Morné likes the game. Sleeping under the table is the de la Rey's normally yapping Pekingese, which has a tiny yellow bow tied behind its head. The patio faces an elaborate rock garden rich with flowers of flamboyant beauty. Presiding over the garden is a purple jacaranda tree. The jacaranda, like the Afrikaner, was an immigrant to South Africa that thrived in its new environment. Jacarandas arrived from Brazil about a century after the white man, and the tree's winged seeds, which can float for great distances, enabled it to conquer the Transvaal.

Suddenly, Morné sits up, attentive. A pleasant, high-pitched note echoes across the patio. *Too-de-lute. Too-de-lute,* and then a slightly different one. *Tee-de-leet. Tee-de-leet.*

Morné listens closely.

"That's a blue asper," he says. "That other note, the higher pitched one, is a Sotho bu-bu."

Morné is an amateur ornithologist. He keeps a pair of binoculars beside him when he is outside. Of the 887 species of birds in South Africa, Morné says, nearly 300 can be found in the western Transvaal and perhaps 100 will flit through his own backyard. The family's thick tome of *The Birds of South Africa* is filled with Morné's jottings.

He watches an olive-colored thrush which is dipping its head in the fountain as if it were a symphony conductor taking bows after a performance. Its place is taken by a brilliant red-billed fire finch which flutters its wings in the water, enveloping it in a halo of mist.

Morné remembers exactly when his fascination with birds began. "It's strange, really," he says. "My father is interested in nature, obviously, and in most cases the son might just follow suit. But it was different with me. All the boys in South Africa have windbuks. It's a small gun that shoots pellets. You don't need a license for one. I was about eleven, and I used to shoot every bird I could. Mostly sparrows and a few doves.

"The sparrow is so common. No one really cares for it. Anything small and dull and brown, people call a sparrow. The English sparrow arrived here on trading ships. Now they're so many of them, and they're a nuisance.

"One day, over there where the bulls are, I saw what I thought was a sparrow, and I shot it. I went over to pick it up. But it was a

starling, a plum-colored starling. I looked at it very closely. I saw
how beautiful it was. The colors and all. From then on, I decided to
look at birds rather than shoot them. I won't even shoot a sparrow
now."

Morné looks like his mother's son, but he wants to be a veterinarian like his father. He says that after qualifying he intends to
get involved in wildlife preservation. Morné is Head Boy at Brits
High School and is considered the very model of the well-rounded
student. "I suppose if all the different types of guys in my school
were put together," Morné says, "I might be the person who comes
out. I may not be the best at anything, but I am good at everything.
I was second in line for the sportsman's cup, second for cricket cup,
and I was class salutatorian."

Students are nominated to be Head Boy by the teachers. Only
the male students and the teachers vote. Teachers' votes are more
heavily weighted than those of the students. "The teachers get who
they want," Morné says.

The Head Boy has a variety of duties. He and the prefects must
be at school at seven to check the premises for bombs. As the
students file in, he watches to see if there are any unfamiliar faces.
No blacks are allowed on the school grounds except those who
work there; if the Head Boy spies an unauthorized black, he uses
his walkie-talkie to alert the headmaster's office. "It's a system of
control and patrol," Morné says. "It's not that something will nec-
essarily happen, but I think it's good for safety with this ANC
[African National Congress] problem."

Each school day begins with a prayer and a Bible reading. In
the assembly hall, the entire student body stands at attention and
recites the school code.

1. I thank God for giving me life and health.
2. I will not let my parents down, they who protect me and sacrifice so much for me.
3. I will strive to live a clean and noble life, and I will set high
   standards for myself.
4. I will keep the honor of the good name of my family and that
   of my school.
5. I will be polite to my parents and my teachers and all other
   people.
6. I will try to keep my language and behavior under control in
   the classroom, on the sport field, and especially in public.

7. I will protect the property of the school and the school building.
8. I will not neglect the privilege I have to study.
9. I will strive to do my work to the best of my ability.
10. I will see to it that my behavior everywhere and always, even
    when I'm alone, will be stainless.

Each morning, from 9:30 until 10:00, is physical defense. "The
name sounds quite impressive," Morné says, "but they don't really
teach us physical defense. The teachers say we have to be ready.
We practice military drilling, and they give us lectures on things
like how to camouflage yourself."

Morné is slightly more conservative than the average Brits student
just as his father is more conservative than the average man in
Brits. Morné, like his father, supported the new Conservative member of parliament for Brits. Politics is a forbidden subject in school,
but it manages to crop up anyway. Morné's main source of political
information is his father since he does not read newspapers or
watch the news.

"We're not allowed to discuss politics in school," he says, "but
we do talk about it among ourselves. You can tell what people
think. NP [Nationalist party] students will compete against blacks.
If there was a cricket match against a team with a black on it, I
wouldn't play. I don't want to mix with them. Not because of their
skin color. But because they're not civilized. In America, I know,
the blacks are civilized. In some cases, just as civilized as I am. But
it's not the same here.

"NP students want to get the attention of blacks. They will
throw tomatoes at blacks standing on the side of the road. If I throw
tomatoes in the road, I will throw them at whites. That's just the
way I am. It's like my father's example of the fellow pulling a girl's
pigtails in school. He's just doing it to get her attention."

De la Rey comes out to the patio before heading off to visit a farm
outside of town.

He is honored that Morné has chosen to become a veterinarian.
"It pleases any father that a son has so much respect for the father
and his profession that he wants to go into it."

De la Rey knows that Morné probably did not consider other
alternatives. "Our South African way of bringing up children," he

says, "doesn't give much scope for developing their own personality and views. It's not like America in that way. In the countryside, they don't have much freedom at all. In the city they get exposed to more. Our way is for the father to tell them what to think. And usually that is what they do think."

De la Rey believes that many Afrikaner children are *too* much like their parents. Not that he objects to the way the parents are, he just suspects that the children uncritically accept the beliefs of their parents and of authority. He is reluctant to impose his views on his children. He wants them to share his views, but he does not want them to embrace those views simply because *he* holds them.

De la Rey prides himself on being a rational man. He makes decisions based on logic, not emotion. He is a man of science and he applies the scientific method to his personal life. Gather data. Form a hypothesis. Test the hypothesis. If the facts contradict it, toss it out.

De la Rey does not have to worry that his wife will simply echo his opinions. Yelena often opposes her husband on issues. "Yelena is very strong. It's important to persuade her that something is right. But I think my children know that I'm the person to discuss things with. I think they know that I'm fair.

"If Yelena saw that the children broke a cup, she might take out the strap and hit them on the bum. Sometimes I would give them six with the *plakkie* [a wooden mallet], but I'd always discuss it with them before. If I saw them do something wrong, I would usually say, 'Come on, let's talk about it.' They hated that. They'd much rather get a hiding."

●

ADJACENT TO THE BHULAS' dining room table, in a recessed alcove lined with mirrors, stands a small sink. Most of the houses in Primindia have a similar arrangement. Hindu and Muslim custom dictates a thorough washing of the hands before eating. "If possible," says Mrs. Bhula, "you should have a full shower before every meal."

Mrs. Bhula is in the kitchen finishing the preparations for

lunch. As always, she wears a sari. Gita, who favors blue jeans, teases her mother about her wardrobe. Mrs. Bhula has never dressed in anything but a sari since her marriage. She maintains to Gita that she wore pants before she was married. "Ah, it was a scandal," she says. "Everybody talked!"

Gita laughs, insisting that it is impossible that her mother ever put on a pair of trousers. Mrs. Bhula likes to create the impression that she was a rebel before she married. "Yes, I was very free before I got married," she says, nodding her head.

Whereas Mrs. Bhula is a traditional woman who seeks to appear modern, Gita is a modern woman who seeks out tradition. Every Wednesday afternoon she takes classes in Bharata Natyam, an ancient Indian dance that tells stories through movement. Bharata Natyam consists of hundreds of stylized gestures which the dancer must memorize. Gita has only learned a few dozen so far. It will take four years, she says, before she can perform a single dance.

For lunch, Mrs. Bhula has prepared *whal-dal*, a dish made of lentils and spices. Jai sometimes finds it a bit bland and he dollops some of his mother's homemade atchaar on it, which he prefers to the store-bought variety. Mrs. Bhula has also made a curry using guvhar, a type of small, thin green bean grown in Natal.

The Bhulas are vegetarians. Gita and Jai eat eggs, but Mrs. Bhula will not. Mrs. Bhula served meat in her house when her husband was alive. "My husband wanted to eat some kind of meat every day," she says. "So I prepared it for him. He liked it. But I never ate it. You shouldn't eat meat of any kind. But today everybody eats it. It's not meant for human consumption. To kill the flesh, no. The purer the food you eat, the purer you are." For Mr. Bhula, eating meat every day was a sign of prosperity. Jai ate meat while his father was alive, but gave it up after his father's death.

Jai's central plate is ringed by a constellation of smaller ones. He uses his right hand to take food from the smaller plates and place it on the larger one. He then takes a piece of *roti*, folds it in half, and dexterously sweeps some curry into it.

"You know," Jai says, "I don't think whites realize that we Indians eat with our hands." Whites, he says, often criticize the black man for eating with his hands, but not the Indian. "Actually it takes a great deal of skill to eat properly with your hands. I remember once, when I was a boy, we ate at a relative's house and

they had a white man over for dinner. We watched him try to eat
with his hands. He held the food up and dropped it into his mouth,"
Jai says with a smile. "It was very entertaining for us."

Jai looks forward to lunch all morning, and then when he actually sits down to eat, he rushes through it. It is as though he feels
he must deprive himself of the pleasure. If he took his time and
lingered, as he would like to, it would reveal to his mother and
sister that he did not want to return to the shop. Jai may be sup-
porting them, but he does not want them to think that he is suffering in order to do so. Jai almost always rises from the table with
food left on his plate as though it were evidence of self-control.

While Jai is finishing lunch, Shamu is in the kitchen begging
Mrs. Bhula to be able to go into the dining room. Mrs. Bhula tells
Shamu not to disturb Jai. But he is insistent and grabs Mrs. Bhula
by the hand, saying, "Come, Ma. *Come*, Ma." Shamu is a tiny
tyrant. No one except his own mother can resist him.

Shamu sticks his hand into Jai's pocket to feel for his keys.
Shamu is fascinated by keys, and will reach into the pockets of
perfect strangers in pursuit of a set. If he finds some, he cries,
"Sharp!" Shamu speaks English with the slight lilt that character-
izes the speech of Brits's Indians. Mrs. Bhula chatters to him in
Gujarati, Jai talks to him in English, and his mother yells at him in
Tswana.

Shamu's arrival at the Bhula household was unheralded. Julia had
been working for Mrs. Bhula for several years. She is a large woman,
with a deep chest and a generous belly. She rarely speaks.

"One day," Mrs. Bhula recalls, "Julia said to me, 'Come into
my room, I want to show you something.' I went over to her bed
and there was a tiny baby bundled in a pretty white embroidered
cloth. It looked like a loaf of brown bread wrapped in paper. I said,
'Julia, whose baby is that?' She said, 'It's mine, Ma.'

"I said, 'Julia, don't joke, whose baby is it?'

'Mine, Ma,' she said.

"At first I did not believe her; I thought she was hiding something. I said why didn't you call me? She said it was late at night
and she didn't want to wake me. She said, 'I just prayed to God and
I knew everything would be all right.'

"She had the baby by herself. I told her to stay in bed to rest,
but she said she felt fine, and went out and started cleaning the

kitchen floor. Julia says you're not a real woman if you have a baby in a hospital."

For Shamu's third birthday a few months ago, the Bhulas decorated the dining room table with a cornucopia of childish delights: bowls of popcorn and potato chips; assorted candies and chocolates. Gita baked three different cakes. Balloons hung from the ceiling. Shamu, in a blue baseball hat and white bib, presided over the table in solitary splendor. When he could not eat another morsel, Gita took out Jai's portable cassette player and put on Paul Simon's *Graceland* album. Shamu loves dancing to the song "Diamonds on the Soles of Her Shoes."

Julia is a Pedi and her other children live with her family in a village in the northern Transvaal. She recently told Mrs. Bhula that it was time for Shamu to move home. Shamu, she said, was getting spoiled. He should be with his brothers and learn his own language. No one in the Bhula household wants Shamu to leave, but Mrs. Bhula understands.

Before going back to the shop, Jai stops by to see Ahmed. They had made tentative plans to do something tonight. Ahmed is Jai's best friend and works as a salesman at Hegel's, the largest shop in Primindia. Hegel's occupies three floors of a modest apartment complex where Ahmed and his family have a flat. The rondeval in which the Bhulas once lived was knocked down to make way for the building. Hegel's was modeled after the large white department stores in town, but it seems more like an old-fashioned general dealership spread over three floors.

On the floor where Ahmed works, Jai sees his friend talking to a customer. Ahmed nods, and comes over after a few moments. Ahmed is not suited to be a salesman: he is serious, almost solemn, and wholly without small talk. He speaks in a husky whisper and has a drooping black mustache that gives him a slightly saturnine air. He has been Jai's cohort on the Indian Ad Hoc Housing Committee and in the protests against the election for the House of Delegates.

Jai asks Ahmed if he is going to Joburg tonight. Ahmed says no. Why not? Jai asks. Ahmed smiles and shrugs his shoulders, as if to say it is out of his hands. Ahmed has been visiting Johannesburg, as he puts it, "to find a wife."

In Primindia, arranged marriages are still the rule. Ahmed is twenty-five and a Muslim. His parents would like him to be married. He admits a bit sheepishly that he has succumbed to their pressure.

This week he has two appointments in Johannesburg with families who have eligible daughters. The ritual consists of Ahmed and his parents going to the home of the girl where the girl's parents serve tea. Sometimes the girl will be there, sometimes not. Occasionally he will get a glimpse of her and sometimes, very rarely, he will be able to take a walk alone with her.

If Ahmed expresses an interest in the young lady, his parents will make an appointment to discuss the matter with her parents. If her parents are amenable, they will discuss it with their daughter. She must also agree. Thus feminism advances. Traditionally, the girl had no say whatsoever. Today, the woman has the right of first refusal.

Most of the girls Ahmed meets have been taken out of school and groomed to be brides. They learn to cook, clean, and sew. Usually, says Ahmed, they are extremely shy. Ahmed would like a woman with a bit more spirit, but that is asking a lot. Ahmed doesn't complain: if you accept the premise, you must accept the participants.

In Brits, marriage between Hindu and Muslim is unthinkable. It was not too many years ago that Brits had its first inter-*jati* Hindu marriage. A woman from a higher station in the Vaiśya caste married someone from a lower station in the same caste. The marriage caused great controversy in town and the bride's mother had a nervous breakdown.

Jai is feeling some pressure himself. As the only son, he is very much aware that he is the bearer of the Bhula name. But he will try to evade an arranged marriage, though not because he rejects it as a system. He is a fatalist; the odds of finding someone compatible are so slim anyway, he suggests, that the chances are probably just as good with an arrangement. But Jai has seen too many American movies not to be a romantic. He will wait.

Jai and Ahmed agree to meet at Hegel's at 6:30.

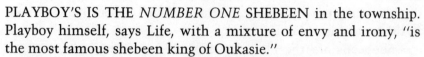

PLAYBOY'S IS THE *NUMBER ONE* SHEBEEN in the township. Playboy himself, says Life, with a mixture of envy and irony, "is the most famous shebeen king of Oukasie."

Oukasie's most famous shebeen king is presently lying fast asleep across the hood of his bruised red Mercedes, which is parked in front of his house. Even when awake, Playboy doesn't say much. He contributes to the air of general good cheer by chuckling at the remarks of his customers.

A dictionary might define a shebeen as a bar or a speakeasy. But that would be like describing a hot dog stand as a restaurant. In Oukasie, a shebeen is simply a house or shack where beer is sold and people drink it. There are no bartenders or barstools, no juke-box and no mixed drinks. People drop by, sit around, drink, talk, and drink some more. If you didn't know better, it would look like a party—which, in a way, it is. No money ever seems to change hands. Music is optional, as are women. But there is always beer.

In the absence of traditional institutions in the township, the shebeen fills the vacuum. Shebeens are meeting places, information centers, sanctuaries. A wife will tell someone at the shebeen to tell her husband that she is going to town; a mother will leave word for her children that she will be home at four; a fellow will announce that he is driving to Pretoria in the morning. There is no newspaper in Oukasie; the shebeen has the latest headlines.

There are about fifty shebeens in Oukasie. The number varies from week to week. A shebeen can open and close in a night. They don't look different from other houses. No sign or license is posted outside. You have to know where they are. Life probably knows the location of every shebeen in Oukasie. He can wander from one to another as though he were just taking a stroll around the neighborhood.

At Playboy's, the men are sitting in the shade of a giant jacaranda tree. The tree's fallen blossoms are scattered like purple confetti at their feet. The air is hot and hazy; everything looks washed out in the brutal afternoon light. The men sit on metal folding chairs and plastic milk cartons. All drink Castle. Life has a half-finished beer in his hand. He is done driving for the day. He dropped off the taxi at Buda's. Buda was not around and Life grabbed two Castles as a reward for the day's work.

Some of the men at Playboy's have been drinking since early morning. Some will remain in the same circle till late in the evening. Two of the men are teachers (they wave hello to their students as they pass); the rest are unemployed. About half the men in the township are out of work.

Shebeens are the blue-chip businesses of the Oukasie economy. As part of its reform policy, the government legalized shebeens in 1986. They work this way: the "bootleggers," most of whom live in Oukasie, buy beer in bulk from the bottle stores in town, where they get a discount. The bootlegger delivers the beer by truck to the shebeens every Friday. Even with the double markup, from the bootlegger and the shebeen owner, people in Oukasie regard it as cheaper to buy beer at a shebeen than to pay for transport into town to purchase it.

Every shebeen has a king—or sometimes a queen. The shebeen king is the host. To be a shebeen king, all that is necessary is the ability to listen to people when they're garrulous, humor them when they're drunk, soothe them when they're angry, and toss them out when they're unruly.

Life was once a shebeen king. He never set out to be one, he just fell into it. He was unhappy with his job at Firestone and he started selling beer on the side to make extra money. His house was large and central; it was a natural place for people to stop.

"I started the shebeen in 1983," Life says. "The money was more than I was making at Firestone. It's not hard to start a shebeen, you know. All you need is to organize a few glasses. Get a generator to play the music. You don't need money because the bootlegger will supply you with the beer and then you pay him back on Monday. You have to spend a little for the ice blocks to keep the beers cold. Control is the most important thing. I always tried to talk to people, find out what they were thinking. As a shebeen king, you never have any privacy."

Life recalls sitting around shebeens as a boy. In the 1960s, it was illegal for a black man to buy beer in a liquor store unless he had a letter from a white man authorizing him to do so. In Oukasie, Life says, only priests and teachers were able to get authorization to purchase beer. Some of the teachers, he says, used to buy a bottle of whiskey, dilute it with tea, and then sell it.

In the old days, shebeens served home-brewed sorghum beer, a dark, bitter-tasting brew. "Very nourishing," Life says. Shebeens also sold mampoer, the potent liquor made from the marula tree. "It was a clear spirit," Life says. "It was very strong and you distilled it in a pipe about two meters long. I used to drink it when I had a cold."

The men in Oukasie drink slowly. The idea is to conserve, to make it last. When pouring, the glass is tilted so that the beer slides in gently without creating a head. A head is wasted beer. One beer segues to another. Bottle openers are not required in Oukasie. One bottle cap is used to pry off another.

The men at Playboy's are discussing the price and merits of various beers. Castle is the *number one* beer in the township. Lion is a distant second. Castle is lionized, Lion is castigated. Such preferences go in cycles; nine months ago, Lion ruled.

The price of Castle has been going up. Life's friend Moshe, a fellow member of the BAC who runs a *kafee* across the way, asserts that the price of Castle is higher because demand is higher. The price of Lion is lower, he says, because it is number two.

"The more people want to buy it," Moshe says, "the higher you can rise the price."

"You capitalist!" Life calls out, and laughs.

One of the drinkers is Godfrey Shongwe, a teacher at Botlabela high school. Godfrey doesn't want his students to see him drink during the week. "Some of the teachers will drink in the afternoon, after school," he says. "There is nothing else to do. But then the students don't like it when you tell them not to drink." Students, he says, come to school hung over. During breaks, they will sometimes go out and buy beer.

"In the old days," he says, "teachers were much older than the students. But today, students and teachers are very close in age. Some are as big as I am."

The members of the BAC often say they want to stop the drinking among the youth, but they hardly set a model example. Some of the youth see the activists as hypocrites in this regard. They drink; why shouldn't we, is the attitude of the youth.

Life does not think much of the present state of schooling in the township. "The schools are no good," he says. "I see that teachers don't even understand the theorems they are teaching. Just because someone is a teacher does not mean he's clever. Students are not taught to understand or analyze. That may be why we don't have any good scientists. Mathematics is a theoretical science. It is just playing with things in your mind. It trains you to think. When I was in school," he says, "I was very good at mathematics."

There are two schools left in Oukasie, a primary school and a secondary school. The primary school has 927 students and the high school, 840. Before the removal effort, each had well over a thousand students. But the South African Department of Education issued a circular which sought to reduce the size of the schools. The Education Department stated that neither school could comfortably accommodate more than 600 students. The overflow, the department said, should attend school in Lethlabile.

Life and the other members of the Action Committee see this as part of the government's removal strategy. "Their idea," Life says, "is that if the child has to go to school in Lethlabile, the parent will think about moving there." It is a clever strategy, Life concedes.

Playboy's sister arrives with some meat for a *braai*. A *braai*, the Afrikaans word for grill, is a barbecue. *Braais* are nonracial, beloved by black and white in Brits.

Life calls for some cardboard to make a fire. A woman fetches some cardboard boxes from inside the house. He takes four bricks and arranges them into a square and then places pieces of cardboard in the center. He lights the cardboard and bends over to blow on the flame.

"We never use wood, just cardboard," Life says. "There's too much smoke with wood and the taste of the meat gets lost." When the fire is burning well, Life places a small, sooty grill across the bricks. He plunks two slabs of meat on the grill, and sprinkles salt —*pours* is probably the more accurate verb—on both sides. Next he douses the meat with red chili powder.

The meat is cooked until any pinkness has been seared to brown. Rare meat is considered uncooked meat. When they are ready, Life picks up the slabs with a fork and drops them on clean pieces of cardboard. In the meantime, one of the women has brought out a large plastic bowl of pap and another bowl of red sauce and onions.

Before eating, a woman with a pitcher pours water onto the outstretched hands of the men, who then rub their hands together and hold them in the air like freshly scrubbed surgeons awaiting their latex gloves. Loaves of bread are brought over and laid on top of newspapers. The men take the loaves, break them in half, and scoop out the dough from the center, disemboweling the loaf. They then pour the sauce along with some of the meat into the cavity.

The men reach into the bowl of pap with their right hands and scoop out a handful, which they then roll into a golf-ball-sized piece. Life is doctrinaire about food. "I don't take pork," he says. "I've never had it. We didn't eat it in my house. It's unclean. I hate fish. You know, if I'm eating fish, I must be desperate." Life eats as slowly as he drinks. He rarely lets food get in the way of talking. Sometimes he uses a fork as a kind of baton to conduct his conversation.

Custom earmarks certain parts of the cow for men and others for women. The hind parts of the cow are for women. Men will not touch them. "I've never tasted that part of the cow," Life says. Liver is for women; kidneys are for men. The tip of the tongue is for women; the back of the tongue, the more tender part, is for men. The head and the neck of the cow, which are highly prized, are reserved for the eldest uncle. The large intestines of the cow are for old women. When passing food, men always pass to the right, women to the left.

Life can explain the source of only a handful of these customs. A woman eats the hind part of a cow and a chicken, Life says, because she lies on her back during sex. If a young woman eats the large intestines of a cow, she will risk becoming barren. In general, though, the cuts of meat which the men don't eat tend to be the least tasty pieces.

The women do not complain. Women in Oukasie are expected to be modest. The woman does not speak until the man does. A woman must not look directly at a man—such a glance is considered bold. A woman is always supposed to keep her head covered when meeting a stranger. It is also important, Life says, for a woman to keep her legs covered. If a man stumbles upon a woman who is undressed, she will cover her thighs. That is considered the most intimate area of a woman's body and the region men find most desirable.

Public affection between men and women is considered unseemly. The men would not think of it, and the women do not expect it. A man and a woman touching each other in public, Life says, is disrespectful. Holding hands would be demeaning to the

woman and emasculating to the man. In Oukasie, women hold
hands with women, and men with men. Schoolboys will routinely
hold hands with each other. Sometimes, when Life is walking
through the township with a friend, they will lightly rest one hand
in another.

Life is very much against "women's liberation." Women have
too much freedom today, he says, and it is all because of the influence of America and the West. "The old ways are better," he says.
"Women have to accept it. The man should control the home. If
you find a family where the lady is in control, it is very embarrass-
ing to the community. Women's liberation is uncultural. It's not
practical here. Women are raised to *work*," he says firmly.

When they are finished eating, the men switch to drinking cane, a
clear, syrupy liquid made from molasses. The standard way to
drink it is to pour two fingers of cane followed by four fingers of
milk. Moshe is particularly fond of cane, in part because the
drinker can pretend to others that he is quaffing down a glass of
milk. Because cane is drunk with milk, people think it is good for
ulcers. Ulcers are common among men in Oukasie. "I think everyone is suffering from them," says Life.

Life lights a postlunch Rothman and tosses a bone to a mutt
they call Feinky. Feinky is the nickname of a local policeman who
is well known in the township. "If this dog were as smart as
Feinky," says Life with a smile, "he would still be too dumb to
pass standard one."

●

ON HIS WAY TO A FARM on the outskirts of town, de la Rey
drives through the residential area of Brits, passing the pretty,
ranch-style houses, with picture-glass windows and lush gardens of
cacti, acacia trees, bougainvillea, zinnias, and marigolds. Garages
in Brits are never hidden; they face the street as though they are
display cases for the cars inside. It is a very neat town. A worker is
always available to clean the streets, mow the lawns, wash the
windows.

In Brits, the wall makes the house. No home is complete with-

out one. Most are made of concrete. Some are decorative; three or
four feet high, with a simple design. Some are protective: six to ten
feet high, topped by electrified wire. Many seem to exist merely to
separate one man's land from another's.

Brits Concrete Walls is located at the very end of Tom Street.
Everyone in town orders walls from here. Anna, the saleswoman,
says the most popular type of wall is plain concrete with horizontal
panels. The second most common type is the "necklace" model,
which has loops across the top. Other popular ones, she says, are
red brick, imitation stone, and white brick. Business, she says, has
never been better.

De la Rey leans forward when he drives. His arms cover the steering wheel as though he were protecting it or himself. He was in a
bad car accident a few years ago, and drives more cautiously now.
Even so, he regularly exceeds the speed limit by a healthy margin.

By Brits standards, however, he is a Sunday driver. The whites
here practice Darwinist driving, the survival of the fleetest. They
don't like it when others pass them by, and will shake their fists at
the offending motorist. Tailgating is the way one car follows another. A yellow light means accelerate in order to beat the red one.

People here care about roads. Proposals for new roads are discussed in detail in the local newspaper. The roads themselves are
built carefully in layers of granite and Tarmac, and are meant to
last. Road signs are plentiful and highly specific. Future anthropologists will earn doctorates for deciphering the complicated hiero-
glyphics of South African road signs. De la Rey passes one sign
alerting the driver to an absence of signs: WARNING: NEXT 8 KM
WITHOUT TRAFFIC MARKINGS.

Just outside of town, the landscape is beginning to turn green.
The small farms start at the edge of town. Every winter, farmers
burn away the remainder of their wheat in order to plant a second
crop, usually tobacco. Some burn their fields in order to spur early
grass and prevent soil erosion when the rains come. Burning the
fields is faster than clearing them, but the charred stubble gives the
landscape a ravaged, post-Armageddon quality, a sense not of re-
newal but of destruction. Now the green shoots are growing over
the stubble. Rain causes the stalks to spring up as if in fast forward.

De la Rey drives parallel to the Magaliesberg Mountains which
are shaped like a great chain of linked sausages. Microentrepre-
neurs haunt the side of the road. An old black man in a blue jump-

suit has set up a flimsy stand. Next to it he has propped up a cornstalk to let passing motorists know what he is selling. A dozen ears go for R2. A boy, no more than eight or nine, holds a ratty umbrella leaking sunlight.

The entrance to the farm is a long dirt road. The Mercedes is jostled by the bumps and de la Rey makes a halfhearted effort to avoid them. The farm spreads out over a series of hills. The house is adjacent to the barn, and next to the barn is the cattle kraal.

The farmer still grows tobacco. When he started farming twenty-five years ago, Brits was the tobacco capital of South Africa, producing nearly two-thirds of the Republic's crop. Magaliesberg tobacco, as it was known, was considered particularly fragrant.

Tobacco is planted in September and harvested in January. The seedlings take three months to germinate, and only then are transplanted to the land by hand. Hailstorms, a perennial hazard in Brits, can devastate a nascent crop.

The farmer reaps the tobacco, cures it, and dries it. The leaf is a light green-yellow when harvested, and turns a deep, golden yellow when dried and cured. There are three principal types of tobacco: lemon tobacco, orange tobacco, and mahogany tobacco. Lemon is the dominant type; manufacturers want 60 percent lemon.

Beginning in the 1970s, the quality of Magaliesberg tobacco deteriorated. The tobacco companies complained. The leaf was not burning properly; inhaling it was a chore. The color was dull; the aroma was off. Farmers were mystified.

Chemists discovered the problem. The water the farmers were using to irrigate their land was polluted. Most of the local farmers used water from the Hartbeespoort Dam, where Johannesburg dumped its waste. Chlorides used to purify the water were contaminating the tobacco.

In 1979, the tobacco companies informed the farmers that Magaliesberg tobacco was no longer up to snuff. Some farmers switched to other crops, some found alternative ways to irrigate their land. Many went bankrupt. In 1979, there were 800 tobacco planters in the area. In 1987, there were 270. In 1982, the area produced 5.7 million kilograms of tobacco; in 1987, 2.5 million.

Farming in Brits is an arduous business. Crop prices have risen by almost 250 percent since 1975, but the cost of farming has gone up by 350 percent. The old days of gentleman planting are over. A local joke: What is the fastest way to make a million rand? Invest two million in a farm.

The farmer and his wife are waiting when de la Rey emerges from the car. The farmer's wife, a rawboned woman with deeply tanned skin, is clutching a tiny Chihuahua against her breast. Not long ago de la Rey treated the dog and she wants to show him how well it has recovered. De la Rey nods. She gives the dog a kiss and then hands it to a black boy who takes it into the house.

The farmer is a haystack of a man, with an enormous belly and powerful arms freckled by the sun. His voice is deep and gravelly; trilled R's rumble out of him like thunder. He doesn't say much, but seems glad to see de la Rey. De la Rey is friendly, but not overmuch. He gets down to business immediately, talking while he's changing into his work clothes. The men discuss the weather —too dry—the price of tobacco—too low—but mostly, the farmer asks de la Rey about the cattle. A few years ago, the farmer cut down on his tobacco crop and decided to expand his livestock. De la Rey describes the cattle operation here as "primitive."

De la Rey takes a blue metal folding table out of the trunk and sets it up next to the car. He places his black medical bag on the table and opens it, arranging syringes and tubes and scissors on the surface of the table. The farmer and his wife seem transfixed by this ritual.

The local farmers often seem in awe of de la Rey's learning. What he does seems strange and magical. In Brits, advanced knowledge and technology are imported, not homegrown. When it is mentioned that someone is learning about the latest advances in some area of science or agriculture, that person is always said to be "studying abroad."

The farmer's workers have lined up nine cows at the front end of the uneven kraal. The sky is cloudless and without end. There doesn't seem to be a shadow anywhere on God's earth. The farm boys are all wearing two or three layers of ratty cotton shirts as though they were afraid of catching a chill. The explanation is simpler: they always wear everything they own.

As de la Rey inspects the cows, a young black boy of twelve or thirteen holds the animal's tail. The boy does not appear to have had a bath in months—if ever. His arms, legs, face, clothes, hair— which sticks up in little koppies—are covered in dust and are a mottled grayish brown.

The farmer informs de la Rey that the black fellow who normally handles the cattle is at a local hospital with his wife. She is having her twelfth child, all of whom live here on the farm. De la Rey and the farmer shake their heads ruefully. They know the story well. The farmer has about fifty workers whom he provides with room and board. Because he feeds his workers, de la Rey says, he can pay them less. And the less you pay them, he adds with a smile, the harder they work.

To harvest his tobacco crop, the farmer brings in workers from the homelands. "Mostly I get women," the farmer says, "not men. Women don't use up the money while they're here. The women plant, reap, sort tobacco. They load manure. They do everything. They work better than the men. Some of them come back for ten years. Local labor stays only a few months. But the homeland workers come back every year.

"Many of the blacks on my farm have been here all their lives. About thirty percent of the workers are on the premises. Sixty percent come from other places. Four times a year, we take them back to their homelands. Sekekuneland. Venda. On Christmas and Good Friday. It's costly to do it, but they're still cheaper than home labor. I prefer the more ignorant black than the more civilized one. I can teach a black woman who can't speak a word of Afrikaans how to grade tobacco in half an hour. The educated ones only bring unrest. I tell you, if the farm workers form a union, it will put them all out of work."

The farmer was born and raised in Brits. Farming is in his blood. "My father was an ostrich farmer in the Cape," he says. "He sold the feathers to London. The feathers were used for clothes, for hats; they were very luxurious. It was a good business, but then the London market for ostrich feathers fell off. Fashion changes. That was 1923."

His father moved to the Brits area and was given a farm of thirty-four acres as part of a government program to help "poor whites." But there was a catch: he had to clear the bush and farm the land by himself, without black help. If he proved that he could do it, he was able to purchase the land for £625.

"People had three or four children. Only the one who couldn't learn, the stupid one, stayed on the farm. But that was the wrong way round. I wanted to go on to university but my father got sick, so I didn't have the opportunity. It was a hard time.

"I farmed tobacco and sold it to the co-op, The Magaliesberg

Tobacco Corporation, the first farmers' cooperative in South Africa. It was started in 1906. The tobacco co-op was formed because the Jews paid the Boers next to nothing for their crop. The Jews would give them groceries for the tobacco. We used to help each other fill a barn of tobacco. Two or three farmers with their children. Not today. Today, the young Boers don't get out of the *bakkie* [truck] when they're farming.

"Today the sewage water in the dam is a big problem for the tobacco. Chloride. Nitric soda. Phosphate. You can't produce good tobacco. They use chloride to kill the bacteria. If the tobacco has too much chloride it won't burn. You can strike a match and it won't burn. If the percentage is over 3.5 it won't burn. The manufacturer wants 2.5. It's very difficult to get that in a dry season."

De la Rey bends his knees slightly before plunging his hand into the anus of each cow in turn. The Dust Boy's eyes widen. There is no water around, so de la Rey can't rinse his arm off between cows. He just holds it away from his body, like a baseball pitcher protecting his arm between innings. These are not show cattle, but carrier cows, and he is trying to discover whether the cows are ovulating. "It's a dirty job, eh?" he says with a crooked smile.

"Putting your hand in here is like putting it in a motor tube," de la Rey says. "There's a vacuum, and it sucks your hand in and makes it hard to work with the uterus. I feel for the ovaries; on it there is a little gland that secretes the hormones. Most vets use rubber gloves, but I think you lose a lot of feeling that way."

As Dr. de la Rey probes each cow, he tells the farmer and his wife about the health of the animal and whether or not it is fertile. The farmer's wife has a dog-eared spiral notebook in which she carefully notes everything de la Rey says.

All the cows are ovulating. He pronounces each fit for carrying embryos. "That's very rare," he says. "Usually, if you have eight, maybe five are suitable." The criteria for good carriers are several. "First, she must be fertile. She must have a frame for easy births. She must have enough milk to raise a calf, and she must be a good mother. How do you tell a good mother? You can tell a good mother from observation. If a dog comes near her calf, she will stand in front of it to protect it. When it's cold, she will lay down on her side to keep her calf warm. You get to know which cows are good mothers and which are not. It's not so different in humans, eh?" he says.

De la Rey believes that blacks are generally not good parents. To him, the fact that black women routinely have babies out of wedlock proves that they cannot be good mothers. "Look, blacks have a child first, and then get married. Moral standards, which we base on our religious beliefs, create social structures that protect the children born in our society. They do not have those standards. Because of our moral standards we help them care for their children."

De la Rey says he looks after such children not because he personally cares for them, but because he is a moral man. What difference does it make why he does it as long as he does it? It is more important to care for the sick than to feel sentimental about them; most people, he suggests, simply feel sorry and don't do anything.

"If you think there is a bad relationship between the blacks and me, you're dead wrong. You can ask any one of my blacks whether or not they are treated well. We once had a farmers' day in the northern Transvaal. The organization included black farmers. I taught them how to give injections, how to analyze dung for disease, and so on. If I minded, I would not have done it.

"The chap who works in our garden has a son, eighteen years old, and we caught the son stealing bags and selling them to the Indians, to International Bag Buyers. He went to court and he got six strikes with a cane. The father said to me, the son is giving me trouble, would you take him to work on the farm? I didn't want to hire him, but because the father had worked for me for a long time, I said I'd give him a chance. But then he pitched off and didn't work. Even his father said he's bloody lazy and doesn't want to work.

"A lot of my blacks have children who work for me. They either go to school or work. Every person in this life has got to know that he's got to work if he wants to live. I work with them. I just don't want to live with them.

"You see, I'm a racist," de la Rey says and chuckles. "I say that in an ironic way. In my own heart and mind, I don't think I am a racist. I think a racist is someone who hates the other person, someone who won't grant the other person his own. I don't think we South Africans are like that." To de la Rey, racism is actually a scientific term that simply means that different races have different characteristics. People in the West, he says, are afraid to acknowledge such differences.

. . .

The farmer's wife brings out a pitcher of lemonade and some cookies. De la Rey helps himself to a glass, careful to use only his clean
hand to pour and drink the lemonade.

As de la Rey changes from his work clothes, a wizened black
man approaches him. He is the embodiment of Yeats's definition
of old age: a tattered coat upon a stick.

"*Baas,*" he says, "I am having a problem." The old man tells
de la Rey that he's lost his pass. He says he went to the authorities,
and they told him that he didn't need it anymore. But, he says, he
still needs his pass because he doesn't want to get in trouble with
the authorities.

"Please, Baas."

De la Rey says that passes are no longer required by law.

"But I must have my pass, Baas," he says.

When he's ready to go, de la Rey puts all his equipment in the
trunk, shakes hands with the farmer, and drives off. The farmer and
his wife wave good-bye and stand in the road as he drives away
across the countryside. It is an Afrikaaner custom to watch your
guest until he is out of sight.

●

JAI'S UNCLE IS BEHIND THE COUNTER when Jai returns from
lunch. He raises one eyebrow when Jai walks in. Jai ignores it.

His uncle has already lowered the brown-and-white awning in
front of the shop. The awning provides a few feet of shade for the
sidewalk and is meant to protect the merchandise in the window
from the afternoon sun. But the merchandise in Bhula Prema and
Son's window—like the goods in all the Indian shop windows—
already appears faded. It is as though the shopkeepers use their
windows not as a display to entice the customer, but as storage
space for goods they have had trouble selling.

Outside, Henry is polishing Mr. Prema's BMW. Henry takes
turns; one day, the BMW, the next, Jai's Mercedes.

Jai's uncle is a naturally diffident man who decided he needed to be
more outgoing to succeed; a Mr. Inside struggling to be a Mr. Out-

side. When people he knows come into the shop, he makes a great display of friendliness. But his affability is gauged to color: he is warm with whites, perfunctory with Indians, and impatient with blacks.

Mr. Prema was liberated by the death of Jai's father. Mr. Bhula had been the dominant of the two, making all the decisions and lording it over his brother a bit.

During the day, Jai and his uncle say little to each other. Their conversation is almost always related to business. His uncle will call out questions to Jai; he will hold up a dress and ask Jai the price. The two never discuss politics.

Mr. Prema thinks that Jai's notion of having more fashionable items could backfire. You need sophisticated customers to have sophisticated merchandise. "We accommodate ourselves to people's demands," he says. "Some of the customers are very fashion-conscious. Some are not. Blacks will buy more blankets in the summer than in the winter. They think they are saving money, but the price is the same."

Mr. Prema is a practitioner of the hard sell. Two teenage black girls are studying a rack of dresses. Jai is in the back. Mr. Prema snaps his finger to get the girls' attention.

"Hey!" he says eagerly. "How about this?" He holds up a blue-jean dress. The girls shrug.

He leans across the counter, slightly bug-eyed, and thrusts a second dress at them.

"How's this?"

The girls look at each other. A minute or two later when they stroll out of the shop, he calls out, "Come here! Come here!" and holds up still another dress. They don't look back.

The slender middle-aged black man who walks into the shop knows precisely what he wants: a khaki, epauleted, gold-buttoned jacket. Mr. Prema looks lost, but Jai digs one out from the back of the shop. It is the uniform of the Zion Christian church, a fast-growing, conservative black denomination that is building an enormous, candy-colored church just over the border in Bophuthatswana. He shows Jai the various medals that he will pin to the jacket. He's on his way to Pietersburg for the annual convention. Last year, two million blacks attended a celebration of the seventy-fifth anniversary of the church. The guest speaker was the state president, Mr. P. W. Botha, who was awarded a medal of honor and commended the church for respecting order, group identity, and authority. The church is a strong supporter of the Nationalist Party. "God bless you," he says to Jai, as he is leaving.

Jai's uncle feels slighted by both whites and Indians in Brits. Each has injured him in different ways. "The Afrikaner is color-conscious," he says, "and he holds the key to the gate. If we had access to the white area, we would kick them in the ass. But he doesn't let us. Why must they be so scared of competition? If you know your business, why be scared? The Indian people, you know, are a business people.

"There is too much competition here in Brits. The Indian area is not well-planned. In the white area, they regulate it so that everyone can make a living. Here they give everyone a license for everything. Everyone's selling the same thing and we're killing each other."

He feels that whites shun him in public, and then entreat him in private. They are eager for Indian shopkeepers to buy land in the CDB through the nominee system. "The white shopkeepers, you know, they come to me and say, 'Eh, Prema, there are so many opportunities in the CBD. What do you say?' But they want money up front. They want monthly and yearly royalties. It is very risky. Then he holds the keys. He gets fifty-one percent and he can claim fifty-one percent of the goods. Then where do you stand?"

At the moment, though, Mr. Prema is more concerned with buying property in Primindia. He recently qualified to purchase a plot in extension 26, the government land extension which is the first development in Primindia since 1972. Those who build a home for less than forty thousand rand qualify for government subsidies. But Mr. Prema has a grander plan in mind. He has been living in a cramped flat on Tom Street for many years and he has saved enough money to build himself a fine place, his dream house. Like his brother, he has hired an architect from Pretoria. "I've waited thirty years," he says.

He is achieving what he has long wanted, but he is still anxious. He believes the situation in South Africa is deteriorating. "After making a few concessions," he says, "things are getting stricter. Look, we were brought up here. We are here for three generations. My father had shops in India and here. But now we have no shops in India. We've got nowhere to go. There are problems everywhere. India is overcrowded. We are better off here."

A short, bustling Indian fellow strides into the shop. His outgoing manner belies an off-putting appearance. He has thick horn-rimmed glasses and oily, wavy hair. He lugs a bulky suitcase that seems to weigh as much as he does. A traveling salesman.

He greets Henry and makes a deep bow to Mabel. She puts her hand over her mouth to hide a smile. He is as ebullient as a Las Vegas stand-up.

"How are you, my friends?" he says.

Jai nods hello. His uncle is more cordial. The salesman has been here before; his territory runs between Rustenburg and Middleburg. They make desultory talk about the weather.

"Ah, it's very hot," the salesman says.

"Very hot," Mr. Prema replies.

"It may get hotter," says the salesman.

"Yes, hotter," says Mr. Prema.

The talk turns to business.

"Did you hear about the school in Laudium that changed its colors from white and gray to blue and orange?" the salesman asks. It sounds like the beginning of a joke, but he is not jesting.

"Well, they did, and without any warning. I know a bloke who already had made up all the uniforms for this year. Now what is he going to do with them? I told him, why didn't you wait to see what they would choose? In the old days, uniforms were always the same. Now, they change them. The black schools had bright colors. The Indian schools usually the same dull colors, white and gray. I tell you, man, it's an uncertain market nowadays. Schools are changing their colors, like that," and he snaps his fingers.

He shakes his head. Jai listens politely, not saying anything. Mr. Prema nods his head sympathetically. The salesman switches to another topic. "Have you heard about the new duty on boots?" He takes out a leather work boot from his satchel.

"They cost me five rand and the duty is seven rand. They come from Taiwan, man. You know, I don't sell fashionable things. I sell to the African. A boot like this is not just a one-season boot. But all they want to know is the price, not the quality. And if I don't have the price, no one buys from me. The women and children, man, they want something new every year. They see a friend wearing something, and they want it too. As for me," he says, pointing to his own clothes, "on Christmas Day next year, I could be wearing this shirt and these trousers. It doesn't matter to me."

Although the salesman is Jai's age, he is of Mr. Prema's era. He takes out pictures of some drab, cheap dresses. Jai looks them over. It is precisely the kind of stuff he wants to get away from. Mr. Prema nods appreciatively.

The salesman reminds Jai of his father's generation; aggressive men for whom business was the entire world. His attitude toward the salesman reflects the same ambivalence he feels about his father and his uncle.

Now that the salesman has finished his pitch, all the air seems to go out of him. His confidence, put on like a flashy suit, has vanished. He runs his hand through his hair, and says he must be going. Jai has already retreated to the back room when the salesman makes his exit.

●

NOT LONG AFTER HE MOVED TO BRITS, de la Rey was approached about running for the Town Council. At the time, Brits was divided into three areas, and each elected three representatives to the Council. Those who sought him out lived in Onderdorp, an area of only a few blocks in the northwestern part of town, the oldest and poorest part of Brits. Onderdorp did not have paved roads, sidewalks, or electricity.

"People came to me to run," he says. "They knew I would do something. But I took it on one condition: that I didn't have to go from house to house to campaign. I never went to one house. I got ninety-nine percent of the votes."

The Town Council, assisted by a host of civil servants, decides virtually everything that happens in town. A tree is not planted that the Town Council does not know about. Their budget is financed from local taxes on basic services: land, electricity, water, roads, and the council appropriates the money as it sees fit. Onderdorp got its paved roads, sidewalks, and electricity.

De la Rey says he was neither liberal nor conservative on the council; his decisions had nothing to do with politics. He advocated things that made sense to him. He was responsible for getting the funding to build the Brits sports center. He also started the town's Parks Department, which today has an annual budget of over 2 million rand. But he did not win every fight.

De la Rey opposed the site of the Indian extension. He was not against an extension per se, but against the placement of it. He was on the subcommittee of the council responsible for planning the extension. For years, Indian leaders had been pleading for more residential and commercial property. De la Rey was unsympathetic. The entire Indian business district, he points out, was then owned by only a dozen families. "They were exploiting their own people," he says.

He proposed that the Indian area be extended to the east, but the Town Council feared the Indians would use the land for business. De la Rey wanted the council to buy his land for the Indian extension. "Then they decided to extend it to the north, toward me, and I had to disqualify myself because I was affected. Although the land where my farm is now would be a natural area for the Indian extension, they didn't want to do it because they didn't want the Indians to be able to open shops along the Pretoria Road. They thought this would give them a big advantage. My farm is to be private in perpetuity, because they want a white buffer between the road and Primindia."

What to do about the Old Location? That was by far the most vexing problem addressed by the Town Council. Ever since the late 1950s, the council had resolved that it should be moved. But where?

"First, you must know the history. The whole development of that township took place illegally. Blacks who came to work in the town needed a place to stay. Out of necessity, they just started to build there. It was difficult to stop them. Say you've got a business in town and you have one or two employees and one or two servants at home—you can't tell them not to build a house. Where would they live? They had to live somewhere.

"Labor increased in town. A few better houses were built in the location. But all this time, the town must be thinking that a piece of land had to be given to them. That's our country. Blacks cannot live in a white area. They were squatters and the council did not want squatters. Squatting is not an accepted form of habitation in the civilized world. The town, as far as its moral obligations were concerned, was trying to assist people who lived in squatters' conditions to move to a decent place. We just couldn't decide where that was.

"I was on the Development Board and I was also chosen in 1968 as the delegate who went down to the Cape to see the minister in collaboration with Potgieter [Brits's Nationalist MP]. We put pressure on the ministry, and in 1969, that's when the government decided to build a place for them called Mothutlung." But Mothutlung proved unacceptable when Mangope decided that only Tswanas could move there. Another place had to be found.

In 1974, de la Rey became mayor of Brits. The position is mainly a symbolic one, and the councillors take turns serving in the job. But during the time de la Rey was mayor, the need to move the township became even more imperative. The Border Industry area changed the calculus of black-white relations in town.

In addition to serving as mayor, de la Rey was in charge of finding an appropriate place to move Oukasie. He traveled around the municipality looking for suitable sites. He had three criteria: it should be on stable ground where building foundations would not be expensive; it should be near Bophuthatswana; and it should be close enough to Brits to allow for an easy commute. Eventually, the farm Nietgedacht was selected, twenty-four kilometers northeast of town. In 1976, the Department of Bantu Administration purchased four hundred hectares of land as the sight for Lethlabile.

"Why Lethlabile?" says de la Rey. "It was wonderfully situated. We knew we couldn't go into Bophuthatswana. We wanted to, though. We tried genuinely and honestly to find the best place. From Lethlabile, they have access to Bophuthatswana schools and universities. And the best hospital for them is in Ga-Rankuwa. We wanted to have the best road connections to each place. From Lethlabile, one road can go to Brits, one to Ga-Rankuwa, the third to Mabopane. Sewage is easy because of the natural flow of water away from Lethlabile. They get their water from Brits and the dam.

"There were areas closer to the white town where we could have placed them, but to have a black town in the midst of a white town and white farms is undesirable. Why was it built there? I shouldn't say this but I'm being honest: we didn't want them close to us.

"Lethlabile is an international township. It's not proclaimed under the Group Areas Act. If I as a white man want to go to live at Lethlabile, I can. It was built on white land. The people who live there own the land, they have title deeds to it, it is theirs." Lethlabile is one of only a handful of places in South Africa where a black man can own property in a white area. Until 1986, blacks could not own land outside of a homeland.

The deal was settled. Lethlabile—"the township of the future," as government brochures soon called it—was where the people of the location would be moved. It would be their final destination, the last stop in a journey that had begun in the 1950s. Once the decision had been made to move the township, the slow, ineluctable machinery of apartheid began to work. Once Lethlabile was built, there was really no choice but to abolish the Old Location and remove those who were left. Once started, no single person or institution controlled the process and it became virtually impossible to stop.

●

THE DAY AFTER THE BLACK COMMUNITY councillors announced that everyone in the township had to move to Lethlabile, a second public meeting was called at the Catholic church. Some two thousand people descended on the church hall for a rowdy and raucous gathering.

"The question was," says Life, "are people satisfied with the removal to Lethlabile? People totally rejected it. It was resolved that the people had not been consulted. They didn't see any reason why they should move from one shantytown to another."

The Brits Action Committee was formed with two representatives from each of the eight wards. Life and Sello were elected chairmen. All of the men elected were current or former union leaders who had learned their politics from a decade of acquiring power on the shop floor. They were tough, pragmatic, and experienced.

"We thought, where do we start?" Life says. "We don't even have transport to Pretoria." Their initial strategy was to ask the government for more land for Oukasie, generate publicity about a forced removal, and seek help from foreign embassies and other antiapartheid organizations. They first contacted the French embassy, which had helped Oukasie workers during the Autocable strike the previous year. They borrowed a car and drove to the office of the Transvaal Rural Action Committee (TRAC) in Johannesburg, an offshoot of the Black Sash that helped communities fight forced removals. There, they met Alan Morris, a young, idealistic graduate of the University of Cape Town who had just started working at TRAC. Brits would be his first case. Morris put them in touch with Geoff Budlender, a prominent antiapartheid attorney who worked at the nonprofit Legal Resources Center.

A third meeting was scheduled and the BAC distributed pamphlets in the factories and around the township. Three days before the meeting, officers from the Brits special branch informed Life that the meeting had been banned by the district magistrate. "By Saturday," Life says, "people were saying we should have the meeting anyway. Some of the youth said we were collaborators for not wanting to have the meeting."

With Budlender's help, the BAC sent a letter to the chief magistrate asking for permission to hold another meeting at the hall. Two weeks later they received permission. The meeting was scheduled for February.

The meeting was a boisterous one. About eight hundred people attended. Part of TRAC's strategy was to generate as much publicity as possible, and Morris had alerted the local and international media. Suddenly Brits became a cause, a pushpin on the map of antiapartheid politics. "Publicity is what TRAC is all about," Morris says. "During the 1960s and 1970s, hundreds of thousands of people were moved without anyone knowing. It wasn't documented. The government hates publicity. Our weaponry is pretty limited: publicity, foreign pressure, trade union pressure, and community pressure."

The BBC was there as well as other foreign print journalists. The police were out in force. Besides Captain Jubber and the other special branch officers, twenty armed black policemen circled the gathering. The people taunted the black officers for being sellouts.

The reasons for not leaving were clear. Lethlabile was too far away; transport to work in town would be expensive and time-consuming. Lethlabile was literally across the street from Bophuthatswana and would be incorporated into the Bantustan. Finally, Oukasie was home, the place they belonged.

During the meeting, a fire was discovered at Razwinane's shop in the northern part of the township. Razwinane was a town coun-

cillor who had already opened a new store in Lethlabile. The fire
had probably been set by the township youth to punish Razwinane,
whom they considered a collaborator. The police barricaded the
roads near the shop. The youth pelted the police with stones. When
the boys began hurling petrol bombs, the police opened fire. A
number of young men were shot and wounded. "We took the kids
to private hospitals," says Life. "We thought that if we took them
to public hospitals, they would be detained. We learned this from
the 1976 riots."

After the burning of Razwinane's shop, the tension in the
township was very high. Hippos—the nickname for the police's
armored personnel carriers—patrolled the township every night.

Within the first few months of the announcement, many people moved to Lethlabile. Some people were afraid of what would
happen to them if they stayed, and so they left. Some people were
afraid of what would happen to them if they left, and so they
stayed. Some thought the government was making a fine offer.
Most of these people were civil servants. But the overwhelming
number of Oukasie residents were scared and confused and did not
know what to do.

The government had built 170 brick houses at Lethlabile,
which they were selling for R4,000 apiece. These houses were
quickly occupied. By January, all of the town councillors and many
landlords had moved to Lethlabile. Landlords, who owned their
houses but not their land, were offered generous cash compensa-
tions for their homes. When they accepted the money, the houses
were demolished by the local authorities.

In Oukasie, an average of three families lived on each stand.
Landlords allowed tenants to build shacks or small houses on their
property and then charged them rent. The local authorities ruled
that if a landlord moved to Lethlabile, the tenants were not permitted to remain on the property. The government also prevented people from moving onto vacant stands, so many of the tenants had no
place to go but Lethlabile. Eventually a suit was filed by Budlender
on behalf of the Action Committee which forced the local officials
to allocate sites to qualified applicants. He saw, and the court
agreed, that under the law the authorities could not use the power
to allocate housing to prevent people from receiving housing.

The government made the township as hellish as possible.
Garbage pickup and waste removal were virtually halted. Police
were omnipresent. Oukasie was in a state of great anxiety. The

township was divided. Those opposed to the removal were intimi-
dating people to stay; those in favor of the move were pressing
people to leave. Families were split. Life's mother and sister decided to leave. By March, an estimated four thousand people had
moved while four thousand had signed a petition protesting the
removal.

In March, Life's house was petrol-bombed. "I was selling beer at
the time and I had a guy assisting me. It was about one A.M. and I
decided to go to sleep. I used to sleep in the front room, but I went
into the back room to sleep. I was drunk and didn't take off my
clothes. At one-fifteen, he woke me and I found the house in
flames. The bomb was thrown in through the window in the front
room." That same night, Jacob Moatse's house was also petrol-
bombed. "A week after the petrol bombing of my house, we were
washing off the walls. One guy came by and dropped off a few beers.
It was sevenish, just after dusk. It was Moshe, Abel, Sello, and
Mike. A group of kids walked up the hill singing that a policeman's
house was burning. We heard shots coming from the house." Life
went to investigate.

"The house was built of wood. It was going up in flames. I
thought, man, you cannot leave, a house is burning, even though it
was not my responsibility. So we tried to put out the fire. The
policeman was driving around looking for the culprits. When he
saw me, he fired a bullet. He came back and put a gun to me.

"After a few minutes, a bunch of police cars came. Captain
Jubber asked me what I was doing. I said putting out the fire. He
said, Ah, that's a good joke. Then he said, Let's talk. I said we
should talk in the light, in front of everyone. He said, get in the car,
we have all night to talk. *No problem.*" Life says this in a high,
nervous voice, and then laughs.

"Feinky Pretorius was driving. Jubber had the four-wheel-drive
car. It was about eight P.M., and they took me to the mortuary.
They said we'd like to get a tire for you. What is your size? They
took a thirteen-inch tire and said, this one looks all right. Then we
drove off." Life knows tire sizes from having worked at Firestone.
"Necklacing," the infamous mode of dispatching collaborators in
the townships, consists of placing a tire around the neck, dousing
it with petrol, and then lighting it.

"We drove down to the Crocodile River. They asked me a lot
of questions. They asked me who burnt down Razwinane's shop. I

said, I think I know who it was, and they asked me if I would show them. They hit me several times. They tied my hands in front with a very long rope. A guy on either side, five meters apart. They put the tire around my neck. Then they said, No, man, it doesn't fit— too big. And they pulled the tire against my throat and said, 'Tell the truth, tell the truth.' They took a petrol container and asked me what it smelled like. Then they put some in my mouth and poured some on the tire. I thought, I'm going to die.

"But I also thought, Ah, there is a trick I could do. I said, 'Captain, I will tell you the truth. But I must talk to you only. Not in front of the other guys.' He said okay and we got by ourselves. I got down on my knees and said, 'Let Jesus Christ be my witness, I don't know anything.' He kicked me and said don't talk about God here. Then something crackled on the radio and they were called to Oukasie. It was about four A.M. and they took me to the police station and locked me up for arson.

"The next day Jubber came back and showed me the minutes from BAC meetings. He said he had more informers than he needs in Oukasie and advised me to move out of Oukasie before I got killed. I took it very seriously. I knew that there were a lot of people in Oukasie working for the police.

"This depressed me. I nearly left Oukasie. I thought that no matter what we did, the police will get our information. I wondered whether it was really worth it. But then I thought I should not let them stop me.

"On Tuesday morning at five A.M., they told me I could go home. It was very nice to hear that. I went to a butcher and bought some meat. Butchers open very early, you know. And I also bought some cigarettes. It was very nice."

The police dropped the arson charges.

The violence continued. The day Life was released, Sello's house was petrol-bombed and a hand grenade was thrown into the home of Leonard Brown, another member of the Action Committee. The BAC believed that the bombings were the work of black vigilantes paid by the police or the town councillors. On May 27, a homemade bomb ripped through the home of David Modimoeng, a prominent Metal and Allied Workers Union (MAWU) organizer and also a member of the BAC. Modimoeng was badly burned and his wife was killed.

Mrs. Modimoeng's funeral was scheduled for the evening of

June 12. It was planned as a memorial, and a celebration of the tenth anniversary of the Soweto riots. Union members from all around the Transvaal were set to come as well as all of Oukasie. Life was in charge of organizing the event.

The night before the funeral, a police convoy rolled into the township at midnight. The contingent consisted of fifteen flatbed trucks, four hippos, and a half-dozen cars. Most of the BAC members were at a nearby shebeen. The police had a list of the people they planned to arrest and Life's name was reported to be on it. That night the police detained most of the members of the BAC, but not Life.

The next day at noon the government announced a national State of Emergency which gave security forces unprecedented powers to make arrests without charge, and hold detainees without hearings. It was far more extensive and restrictive than the State of Emergency imposed in 1985.

The police outlined a variety of restrictions for the funeral. No procession by foot. No flags or banners. No political speeches or songs. Three thousand people attended. "I couldn't do anything," Life says. "I had to give a speech. I said only two words and started crying. They didn't pick me up, I think, because I was responsible for the funeral. They would get me afterward."

The police came looking for him the next day, but by then he had skipped town. For the next few months, he would only slip into the township at night.

On October 17, Mr. Chris Heunis, the minister for constitutional development and planning, announced that Brits Old Location had been officially "disestablished." Heunis said that "in order to assist these people in moving to the better conditions offered by Lethlabile without delay, I have decided that the black town at Brits is to be abolished." According to section 37 (2) of the Black Communities Development Act, he said, the land occupied by Oukasie "is no longer defined and set apart as a town." He added that the people remaining there were living in "deplorable," "unhygienic" conditions and that the cost of upgrading the township would be "astronomic."

Oukasie no longer existed. Overnight, the ten thousand people who remained were no longer residents of a township but squatters in a no-man's land, subject to prosecution and eviction.

The community held a general meeting the next day and voted

to stage a general strike. Two thousand residents signed an affidavit stating that they had not been consulted and did not want to move. Life was quoted as saying, "The people won't move. They are prepared to die. They [the authorities] are going to have to tear down our houses with the people inside them."

The proclamation seemed to contradict the February 1, 1985, announcement that the government was suspending all forced removals. People had visions of the 1984 removal at Mogopa, when police cordoned off the township in the middle of the night and forced the villagers into trucks. But a ministry official described the situation at Oukasie as a "voluntary removal."

Brits became an international news story. The "disestablishment" made the front page of *The New York Times* and the *Washington Post*. It was featured on two of the three American evening news broadcasts and the BBC. All the stories had the same theme: did what happened in Oukasie presage a return to the era of forced removals?

Forced removals, also known as relocations, are coerced, state-sponsored resettlements of non-whites from white urban areas to the homelands. A group called the Surplus People Project has estimated that between 1960 and 1983, slightly more than 3.5 million people had been forcibly relocated, while another 1.8 million are under the threat of removal. Removals were traditionally the principal instrument of the homelands policy. The Transvaal has had the largest number of removals; an estimated 1.3 million people were relocated between 1960 and 1983. During the 1960s, dozens of townships were "abolished" and the people shunted off to Bophuthatswana.

But then nothing happened. No trucks came. No ministers said anything about Oukasie. The police presence diminished. Things returned to normal.

The BAC and TRAC commissioned and then issued a feasibility study stating that the township could be upgraded, with improved roads, sewerage, and water supply, at an estimated cost of 3,026,000 rands. The government did not acknowledge the report.

In October of 1988, an announcement in the government gazette officially declared Oukasie to be an emergency squatters' camp. And, again, nothing happened.

The government was in a quandary. Oukasie was actually a

remnant of policies which they had abandoned and declared dead. After the 1986 Restoration of South African Citizenship Act allowed some blacks who lived in the homelands to regain their South African citizenship, the policy of moving black towns to the borders of the homelands and then having them incorporated had seemingly ended.

But the removal of Oukasie had begun when those policies were in force. Now, only the Town Council was eager to move the location. For the Nationalists, Oukasie was a troublesome thorn. They had already lost the parliamentary seat at Brits to the Conservatives, so moving Oukasie in an attempt to retain the seat was moot.

But what they had started, they no longer knew how to stop.

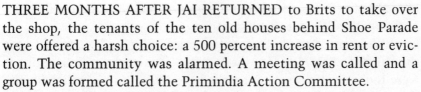

THREE MONTHS AFTER JAI RETURNED to Brits to take over the shop, the tenants of the ten old houses behind Shoe Parade were offered a harsh choice: a 500 percent increase in rent or eviction. The community was alarmed. A meeting was called and a group was formed called the Primindia Action Committee.

"I attended the meeting," Jai says. "I was still feeling new to Brits. I decided to go and keep my mouth shut. There was some movement among young people to try to get land. A petition was drawn up. They came to me for help. I had been involved in some surveying in Joburg and I drew up a survey questionnaire for Brits for housing. I got a lot of students involved." When the survey was complete, the Ten House committee wrote a letter to the minister of housing. The minister stopped all unauthorized demolition of housing in Primindia. "It was a small achievement," Jai says, "but it was nice to achieve something."

Jai was fascinated by the intricacy and ironies of the situation. "This area hasn't increased in size in thirty years, but the population has increased ten or twenty times. When this was declared an Indian area most of the land was already in the hands of Indians. So the landlords became rich. There was an artificial shortage of housing. Here the battle was against the state on the one hand *and* the landlords on the other. That's what made Brits unique."

• • •

In 1985, Primindia was scheduled to vote for a representative to
the Indian House of Delegates, the new entity in the tricameral
parliament created by the government as part of its reform policy.
Jai was opposed to the parliament because it excluded blacks and
assured continued white domination. The United Democratic
Front, an umbrella group of antiapartheid organizations, called for
a national boycott of the election. A candidate for the House of
Delegates was supposed to speak in Brits.

"We thought it was important to take a stand against it and we
did. We distributed pamphlets; things from the UDF. Only forty
people attended the speech. People, I suppose, stayed away because
of the protest. There were security police there. I stood up and told
the candidate why I thought the whole thing was wrong. I told him
that he would be powerless and only in control of small, insignifi-
cant matters. He said no, this is a point of departure. I said people
used that phrase in the past; I said now it was time for arrival.

"Before the election, we put up DON'T VOTE posters. Because
we didn't want to provoke the authorities we investigated the municipal bylaws. They said that the posters had to be stamped by the
municipality. We got them stamped.

"We wanted to have an antielection rally, and we tried to get
the Hindu Indian Hall, but the Indian officials who were running it
were too scared. So we approached the white municipality for the
use of the fire station." Jai smiles at this. "That's the first and last
time something like that will ever happen in Brits. We got permission. We just said it was an election meeting, which it was—an
*anti*election meeting."

Only 13 percent of the eligible voters in Primindia cast ballots
for the House of Delegates election, an even lower figure than the
national average of 16 percent.

When Jai and Ahmed heard about the mass funeral for Joyce Modimoeng on June 12, they decided to go. Neither had ever been to
Oukasie.

"The funeral was in the morning," Jai recalls. "There were
many, many heavily armed police. It was emotionally charged. We
got back by about one o'clock. We heard on the radio that a State
of Emergency had been declared. It was ominous. We had pamphlets for the June sixteenth commemoration [of the Soweto upris-

ing] and the closing of shops on that day. We realized that under the emergency they were illegal, so we burned them.

"On June sixteenth, our shop was closed. An Indian guy from Pretoria or Joburg—I'm not sure which—came to deliver compost to the house. I was in the bath. I got up late that day. While I was outside, ripping open the bags of compost, Gita came to me and said there were police at the door.

"Feinky was there. He just said, we have come to arrest you under the State of Emergency, section three. I was shocked. Under section three, they could hold you incommunicado for fourteen days. They said, all right, take us to your room. They ransacked my closets.

"They would take things out and glance at them and smile, giving each other knowing glances. You'd have thought they had found naked photographs of Bo Derek or something. They found a June sixteenth pamphlet from 1983, and said we intended to distribute it this year.

"They were here for about three hours, going through my things. They made dozens of piles. I had everything here. Pamphlets and petitions from university. Even T-shirts. Things I'd written. They took two big boxes. When Jubber came here, I didn't know who he was. He said something like, 'How the mighty have fallen' in Afrikaans. If it wasn't so serious I would have laughed.

"After all that, they said they wanted to come to the shop. My uncle was there. All my uncle said was, 'You don't have anything here, do you?' My uncle talked to the police about the weather or something. He parted on a good note with them. He asked me how long I was going to be, as if I were going on holiday," Jai says and laughs.

Ahmed had been arrested at the same time. "They took us first to the police station. I went into cell number three, Ahmed into number six. We didn't know the guys from Oukasie had been picked up. The first few weeks we were in solitary. What solitary confinement means is that you're deprived of the sight and sound of other humans. I was kept alone. Entirely, entirely alone.

"At first I would get this hard cold slab of mealie meal. I ate about an eighth of it. I had that for a day or two. I told my warder that I was a vegetarian and I didn't eat anything else and that I would be struck down by the good Lord if I had to eat meat. You know, you can't speak of personal conviction with them; that doesn't carry any weight. You must speak of God. But I'm sure they considered me some kind of infidel who thinks he's got religion.

"Then, suddenly, we began getting food from home. The police station, you know, is not a prison. It's just a temporary holding place. For me, though, it meant something. It symbolized normality. When I ate *roti*, I knew who made it, either my mother or Gita. Gita's *roti* is thinner and more delicate than my mother's.

"I slipped them a message that I was in control of myself. I wrote it in Gujarati. There are very few people my age who can write in Gujarati. I also assured them that if I had been doing in Joburg what I was doing here, no one would have paid attention to it.

"My cell was filthy. I couldn't even go to the toilet the first day, it was so horribly dirty. In detention, we never shaved. There were no facilities for bathing. I told them I was very religious and I had to wash. They only let me bathe in cold water outside. But it's strengthening. For the first three weeks in detention I had the flu. But I've never had the flu or a cold since."

Jai was interrogated by Captain Jubber. Jubber asked Jai about various things that were confiscated from his room. "Jubber kept asking me about the *New Socialist* magazine. He asked me where I got it from. I told him—without being flippant—that I got it at the CNA. He told me to stop lying. Over the next couple of days, he kept harping on the magazine, and where it came from. I said you could buy it at the CNA and that I hadn't even asked them to order it for me specially. A couple of days later, he stopped talking about it and I finally asked him whether he had looked into the *New Socialist* business. He told me not to be a wise guy."

After three and a half weeks, he was allowed visitors. Jai's friend Navine, who worked for a local mining company, would bring Mrs. Bhula every day. "Navine became like another son. Soon after I was held, he called up the police station to check on how I was being treated. You know, he has a very deep, authoritative voice. When Captain Jubber got on the line, he said, '*This is Navine calling.*' Navine just asked how I was doing. When Jubber got off the phone, he came directly to me, and said, Bhula, your family has called a Jewish lawyer. He seemed scared. I said I didn't know anything about such a thing. Jubber told me the lawyer's name was *Levine.* I wracked my brain, but of course I couldn't think of anything. Then Jubber said that if I did not tell my family to have the lawyer back off, he would really make my detention unpleasant.

When I did realize it was Navine who had called," Jai says, with a smile, "I did not tell him."

Prison had its pleasures. "I used to be able to see the rays of the sun. I watched how they illuminated parts of the wall. How the shadows moved. I developed a regime. I would take walks in my mind, imaginary walks. I'd go visit someone. On Friday nights, I could hear the sounds of the Molani disco. I used to go to the outside enclosure and listen to the songs. Like it was a night out in town. To me, it really was that. It's very hard to explain. I attuned myself to a much more low-keyed existence. I had nothing. I said to myself, this is your life, this is your reality. So find your happiness and meaning within the confines of these four walls. I found it stimulating. Which is not to say that I didn't get depressed. I cried. So on Friday nights, when I heard that music, I was filled with joy."

After six and a half weeks, Jai and Ahmed were taken to Pretoria Central Prison. They were still not charged, and under the State of Emergency, they did not have to be.

"We got there and were taken to a big hall where they were processing most of the prisoners. It was there that we saw Sello, Moshe, and the guys from the Action Committee. They told us about a cop at Brits who told them that we were so smart that we could make a bomb in our cells.

"For two days we were in solitary. In detention anything can happen. You can die and they can say you slipped on a bar of soap. The cell was very small. A bed, toilet, and a basin. No windows. No light. We could hear the traffic outside.

"But we wanted to get out of there. They transferred us to the main cell block. There were about five to six hundred emergency detainees, divided into thirty to fifty to a cell. There were no white security prisoners. One toilet. No privacy. But one loses a sense of it. When we walked in we saw people playing chess, others playing cards, a couple of guys reading. We thought, *five-star hotel.*

"Everyone just took to each other. The trade unionists were particularly impressive. There were high-powered, political discussions. People were chanting ANC songs until two or three in the morning. It was all utterly, totally uninhibited.

"Everyone took turns cleaning the cells. It was democratically decided. A prison official would come in the morning. Everything had to be done before the inspection and that was about five in the morning. Someone said to the official: we are not petty criminals here. We have not committed any crime. We are here for political reasons. You should treat us with the respect we deserve. Why don't you say 'Good Morning' to us?

"In prison we were often kind of mediators between the young guys and old guys. The young guys were doctinaire Marxists. They treated Marx as if it were holy writ. They read it literally. I explained that the work had to be adapted to his time. They would say that Marx said man should use science to tame nature and used the example of the lightning rod. But I said that a lightning rod did not tame nature; taming nature would mean getting rid of the lightning altogether.

"I think some of the young Marxists were very naive. They wanted to nationalize everything immediately. Anyone who understands a little about how things work will know that there are no absolutes.

"The guys call prison 'the university.' They say John Vorster prison is the biggest university in South Africa. Sometimes they call themselves 'graduates.' Someone will say, 'I'm a graduate of the *university*.'

"How can they still smile after what they've been through? I know that the little I went through made me bitter. I saw guys who went through a thousand times more than I did, and they wanted nothing for themselves. The whole thing filled me with humility."

One day, a prison official informed Jai that he was being released. He had been there for three weeks. He was never charged.

"The next day after I got out of detention I was in the shop. I didn't mind talking about it. Some people were very disturbed by it and didn't want to talk about it. But I had psyched myself up in prison. I felt stronger the longer I was there.

"To tell you the truth, I feel a lot more corrupt being out of prison than in. You plumb a greater depth within yourself. You had to entertain yourself. I wouldn't say I'm the poorer for it. I would say my quality of life has deteriorated since then."

●

MATELA'S HOUSE IS ONE OF THE OLDEST in Oukasie. Her front yard boasts what is probably the township's grandest jacaranda. It shades the entire house and its roots pop out of the ground like great veins, which function as natural barstools for the men sitting in the yard drinking beer. Life and Moshe adjourned from Playboy's to Matela's, which is at the upper end of Oukasie. Sello has joined them.

Matela is a shebeen queen, a large, proud woman who doesn't say much. Her face, like those of many of the older women in the township, is mottled and blotchy, the result of years of skin lightening creams. Fewer of the younger women are marked in such a way.

Matela comes out of her house and stands with her hands on her wide hips, surveying the scene. "Hello, Ma," Life says, and she nods and smiles. "Matela," Life says, "is not like the other women." Matela is one of the few women activists in Oukasie. In many ways, Life suggests, women were the prime movers behind the migration to Lethlabile.

From the beginning, women seemed to like Lethlabile. They saw it as a better place, and saw no reason—political or otherwise—not to move there if they had the chance. Normally such a decision would be made by the man, but the men hesitated. The women did not; they were determined not to let their husbands' qualms stand in their way. The wives, Life says, could only look at the issue personally, not politically.

"When the men were at work," Life says, "the women would call for the government trucks, move everything to Lethlabile, and then leave a note for their husband, telling him the stand number." Oukasie has few divorces, but the removal split many marriages.

Matela is a member of the People's Court, a shadowy institution in Oukasie. Typically, those who are on it don't talk about it; those who talk about it are not on it. The court was created to sidestep the municipal justice system and avoid getting the police involved in the affairs of the township.

The People's Court blends union structures and Tswana customs. Each of the town's districts is represented on the court by a single member. If someone has a problem, he can request help from the court member in his area. The court will listen to both sides of the story and reach a decision. The court is supposed to be apolitical and above any factional rivalries.

Matela describes how the court works. "Let's say my husband hits me. I go to the member of the People's Court in my area and make a complaint. Then the court will come to see me in person. They will discuss with me what happened, and propose some remedy. The court does not take sides." But the court *does* take sides; they will make a decision as to who is right and who is wrong, recommend punishment and administer it. They have been known to use sjamboks on those they deem malefactors.

Life is leery of the court, but defends it. The people have no choice, he says. "When they took their complaints to the police, the police said: You listen to the Action Committe about Lethlabile, why don't you take your quarrels to them as well. So we took the police's advice. The idea is not to rely on white justice." The notion is to create their own institutions—to literally take the law into their own hands.

The People's Court makes the police uneasy. They consider the court a vigilante organization dispensing frontier justice. Yet many residents of Oukasie also mistrust it, fearing favoritism and spitefulness. They may not have great confidence in the municipal courts, but they are not comfortable casting their lot with the People's Court, either.

The People's Court is not the only homegrown legal institution in Oukasie. There are also the street committees. The street committees were organized by the Brits Youth Committee in an effort to improve life in Oukasie. They patrolled the township, cleaned up refuse, and sought to cut down on drinking. They also created makeshift gardens whimsically decorated with tires and used-car parts and gave them names like Freedom Park and Survival Park.

But the gardens have gone to seed. They look as ragged as the rest of the township. Now street committees roam the township at night. Their objective is to prevent robberies and intimidate informers. But some people, Life among them, wonder whether they are a cause of crime rather than a cure. Others see the street committees as rivals to the BAC.

·   ·   ·

Matela is charging two rand for a bottle of Castle. Moshe rubs his hands in mock glee: "That's what I'll be charging tomorrow."

Life spends most of his money on beer. Drinking, Life contends, is part of his responsibility as a leader. He justifies it on practical grounds. "You can't really talk to people unless you're drinking," he says. "If you go and sit with people who are drinking, and you're not, they freeze up. To really know what people are thinking, you have to be with them at two o'clock in the morning. It's only at two A.M. that they really tell you how they're feeling."

Life sucks the last bit of smoke from his cigarette, and stubs it out on the ground. "I hate smoking," he says, smiling. "I'm very much concerned about my health. I read in an American magazine —*Ebony*—that smoking was a health hazard."

Sello says to no one in particular: "I hope there are no meetings next week. I want to enjoy myself. I think I will drink myself to death. There is no pain that way."

"How do you know if you've never done it?" asks Life.

"I have come close. But I've read that psychologists say that it is true that there is no pain in drinking yourself to death."

"Psychologists deal only with fantasy," says Life.

"Still, compared to other ways," says Sello, "it would be a fine way to die."

●

JAI'S UNCLE ANNOUNCES THAT HE is going to nip out for a few minutes. Every afternoon, he scouts the local vegetable shops for the freshest mangoes, the ripest tomatoes, the sweetest peppers. He is fussy about fruits and vegetables, and likes to find the best to take home to his family.

Moments after Mr. Prema steps out, a blond, mustachioed fellow struts into the store. He sports a watch with a face made from a gold coin and a braided gold bracelet that a less muscular person might find a chore to lift. He greets Jai like a long-lost pal.

He plunks a suitcase down on the counter and lifts the lid with a flourish, as though he were opening a treasure chest. He reaches in and grabs a woman's shoe by its delicate heel and holds it aloft.

"These . . . are . . . *magic!*" he says.

Jai smiles. This fellow is *selling*. Jai has bought from him before, and likes the man's line; the shoes are contemporary and well-
made.

"I'm supposed to be on holiday," the salesman explains in a
strong Afrikaans accent, "relaxing by the pool, you know. But these
shoes are going like crazy, and I wanted to take care of you."

Jai calls over Mabel to have a look. The shoes are pastels:
yellows, pinks, avocado.

"Which ones do you like?" he asks her.

Mabel is his index of popularity: if she likes them, Jai's customers will fancy them. She picks out four pairs, one of which is a
simple brown leather slip-on.

"Too plain," the salesman says.

From among Mabel's four choices, Jai selects all but the brown
one.

The salesman takes out a pair with a big round metal buckle.
"These are flying off the shelves," he says.

Jai nods. He will stick to the three. As the fellow is writing up
the order he tells Jai that he will head back to the beach in a day or
two after he visits all his clients. Business is good. He mentions
that he has just bought a Mercedes for R116,000 and a gold Rolex
for R40,000.

Jai is bemused by the fellow. In the past, the two of them have
even talked a bit about politics. The fellow is reasonable, Jai says.
He shakes Jai's hand, and is off. See you next year, he calls out,
before sliding into his Mercedes.

Jai wouldn't mind becoming more friendly with the salesman. He
has a yearning to show that it is possible for a white and a non-
white to be friends in Brits. Indians tend to romanticize their relationships with whites, mistaking courtesy for understanding and
cordiality for intimacy. Jai does not trust these feelings in himself.
Whites, he says, have always let him down.

When Jai was a boy, a local farmer and his son used to regularly
come into the shop. The son's name was Koos and he was the same
age as Jai. The farmer was not well off and Jai's father occasionally
extended him credit.

"When his father was out front," Jai recalls, "Koos would come
into the back and we would play together among the mealie sacks.
We got to know each other quite well as children. After that, as we
got older, I would see him occasionally around town, and we would

talk. It seemed like we really *could* talk. Sometimes he would use a racial epithet, and I would tell him that I did not like it. He seemed to think that was fine, and stopped using it. He was not very well educated, and I could understand him saying such things. Anyway, I thought that it might be one of those rare friendships between a white and a non-white. Koos didn't go to university. After finishing school, he became an apprentice mechanic at one of the garages in town.

"After my father passed away, when I had all those problems with the Mercedes, I decided to take the car to Koos. He agreed to repair it and he said he would fix it right away. But then he kept it for three weeks. One afternoon, during this time, he and his partner came into the shop and selected things worth about R300. They said they did not have much money on them at the moment, and could they pay at the end of the month. I said fine. That evening I went to see Koos about my car. His partner, I could tell, was very conservative. When I asked him whether Koos was there, he said, 'You mean *Baas* Koos.' Koos came out and he was a bit drunk. I went and looked at the car and I could see immediately that something was wrong. It was damaged. He had drilled holes in the carburetor. I said that I thought something was wrong with the car and that I would take it with me. He said fine, that it was taking up too much space in the garage anyway. It cost me three thousand rand to fix what he had done.

"The mechanic I took it to said not even an apprentice mechanic could ever make such a mistake, and did the mechanic have some kind of grudge against me? He has never paid for the things he bought at the shop either."

When Jai went off to university, his only experience with whites was with Afrikaners from Brits. He knew nothing of white English-speaking intellectuals like the kind he met at the University of Witwatersrand. He admired and emulated them.

"When I was first at Wits," Jai says, "I used to think that if a white person talked to me he was a nice guy, and I would like him. All he might say is, can I borrow your pencil? Or do you know which book the reading is from? And I would feel flattered, honored that he had talked to me."

Jai had decided to study design and become an architect. He could draw, he was good at physics and mathematics, and he liked the idea of building something of his own creation. Still, it was an unusual choice. Indians at white universities like Wits typically selected majors like mathematics or chemistry, objective disciplines that would not put them at the mercy of the subjective judgment of white lecturers. Jai crossed paths with a lecturer whom he found less than impartial.

"I was very naive and vulnerable. I come from a very small town. I didn't know people who went to university. If I was late for class, I would come in the room and say, 'Sorry I'm late, sir,' and people laughed at me for calling the lecturer 'sir.' He played to our sense of insecurity. He would say to the black students, 'Do you understand?' 'Do you get what I mean?' He addressed us as you address a child.

"I don't think I'm being oversensitive. I suppose I'd never encountered a situation like that before. I wasn't in a position to counter him in any way. I allowed myself to be intimidated.

"We had a project called 'My Place.' They took us to a site for which we were supposed to design a house. It was on a hill and was very rocky. I designed a hexagonal house, made of six triangles. I used the rocks that were on the site as a design element of the house. I got completely absorbed in the project. When I get absorbed in something, nothing else matters. When my friends saw the design, they commented on how good it looked. I was quite proud of it. It was a very important project for the class.

"When he gave me a bad evaluation, I nearly cried that day. I thought perhaps I didn't have it in me. I felt everything I had done was so correct. I felt this guy was out to get me. There was no one I could talk to. I didn't know anyone well enough. I felt so cornered. I never knew anyone at university before. Then I dropped out of the course. If you fail design, you fail the whole year."

At precisely 4:45, Gita arrives at the shop with some *cha*, which is an Indian herbal tea, and biscuits. When she comes to the shop, she usually sits with Jai for a few minutes and talks quietly.

Gita recently graduated from Wits. She studied education and commuted from home. She did not try to leave Brits behind when she went to the university. She conscientiously did her work and did not get politically involved. She has applied for several teaching jobs in town and is waiting to hear. When Jai complains of the narrowness of Brits, she sympathizes with him. But she does not feel the same way. Brits makes her brother feel cramped and restless, but she finds its smallness and sameness, its dependable monotony and familiar cast of characters, to be reassuring.

●

DE LA REY OWNS A SECOND FARM—he always calls it his lucerne farm—about half a mile east of his house, on the other side of the Pretoria road. The farm is forty-seven hectares, forty-one of which are under cultivation for lucerne, which he grows to feed his livestock. Whatever is left over, he sells on the open market.

It rained yesterday and he is worried that the lucerne could get waterlogged. He had asked Ben, his foreman, to cut six hectares this morning. After finishing with the farmer's cattle, de la Rey wants to see how the cutting is going. He drives up a snaking dirt road that runs alongside a small stream. The farm is on rolling land, divided into segments by lines of trees and bushes.

"Lucerne is the most desirable of all animal foods," de la Rey says. "The scientific name is *Medicago sativa*. It is known as alfalfa in the States. It's very high in protein, also in vitamin A and carotene. It can be used for all animals. Horses are very keen on it. It's excellent for cattle, pigs, even chickens."

"Lucerne is harvested all year round. Eight to ten times a year. You plant it, you rake it, and you bale it. Simple. One hectare provides six cows with feed for a year." There is only one problem with lucerne, he says. "You need a lot of water to grow it, but a dry day to cut it."

De la Rey bought his lucerne farm to save money, not make it. But the farm has turned out to be lucrative in a way that he did not anticipate. In fact, to call it a gold mine is almost an understatement.

Brits sits atop the Bushveldt Igneous Complex, a vast two-billion-year-old basin of volcanic rock that contains one of the largest and richest mineral deposits in the world. The complex is shaped like an enormous layer cake, narrower at the base than at the top. The heaviest metals are concentrated in the layers at the base. The middle layers contain chromite, platinum, gold, and other metals such as palladium and radium. The topmost layers have seams of chromite, vanadium, and magnetite. De la Rey's farm is part of the icing on the cake.

Ten years ago, a platinum company called Lefkochrysos—"white gold" in Greek—commissioned a geological survey of the Brits area. It was already known that the complex contained 80 percent of the world's known platinum, a metal considerably rarer than gold. Lefkochrysos discovered that a platinum reef dips up just south of the town, covered by only a few meters of black turf. The area offered large, minable blocks of platinum. The only problem was that it was in the middle of a nexus of citrus, tobacco, and vegetable farms, some of which were only a few hectares in size. Mining companies were traditionally hindered from getting access to the land by the complex quilt of small farms. Three years ago, Lefkochrysos established a set price per hectare for drilling and surface rights and began negotiations with each individual farmer. Persistence paid off. Lefkochrysos is the first new platinum mine in South Africa in fifteen years.

The mine will be completely mechanized. Images of black men in overalls carrying picks and shovels are all wrong, says William James, a polished English-speaking Lefkochrysos executive. The company will be using vehicles known as Load Haul Dumpers (LHDs), which cost about R600,000 apiece and resemble muscular caterpillars. The advantages of a mechanized mine are several, he says. It's cheaper because it uses less labor, traditionally the largest expense in mining. The only workers will be the LHD drivers. Brits, he notes, has the reputation of being a strong union town—but there will be no strikes at this mine because there will be no unions.

De la Rey's farm is not near the primary drilling area, and Lefkochrysos offered to buy the mineral rights to his land, which would not affect the surface. He had no problem accepting the money, but he does have larger reservations. "Mining changes a town," he says. "Brits will become more urban. I don't like a city way of life, a city way of thinking. I prefer a country town. I don't need a bloody cinema," he says with a smile. The mining business in South Africa is too slick, too *English* for his taste. Lefkochrysos, like most large mining companies in South Africa, is in the hands of English-speaking businessmen.

"There will be more doctors, more chemists," he says. "It won't mean one more cent for me. In my profession, you earn what you work for with your hands."

. . .

De la Rey drives up to the barn. The tractor is inside. He finds that odd; Ben should have the tractor out in the field.

He drives out to inspect the fields that he wanted cut. They are not and he sets out to find Ben. He does not locate him, but discovers that a different field has been harvested. De la Rey is nettled. He squints up at the sky. The afternoon sun is still high, the deep blue stretching away to infinity. He scans the horizon for clouds. The weather report mentioned a chance of rain.

De la Rey trusts Ben, who is from Venda and in his early thirties. "He's a very good worker," de la Rey says. "I pay him a white man's salary. People pay blacks less in this area. But he deserves what I give him. He knows what to do without me having always to tell him. Without benefits, he gets R1,000 a month. I think he has eight children."

De la Rey also provides him with a small house. The house was part of the property when he bought the land and is quite comfortable.

Near Ben's house are the accommodations for the other workers. Each family is given a brick and plaster house, about 10 feet by 20 feet, divided into two rooms with two small windows. There is running water and a toilet, but no electricity. The houses are huddled up against one another, each with a tiny plot for growing mealies.

De la Rey decides not to search for Ben. It's late, there is no sign of rain, and he will talk to him tomorrow. He takes a different route back to the main road and passes Ben's house. De la Rey says that Ben has electricity in his house, and a TV and stereo. But de la Rey notices that a part of the house he thought was empty seems to be occupied. He does not recognize some of the children running around the yard or the women doing the washing. De la Rey shakes his head. "I told him, no lodgers," he says. "I pay him enough that he does not have to take in lodgers. So why does he do it?" De la Rey accelerates away from the house in a swirl of dust.

De la Rey says he treats his workers as he would want to be treated himself: fairly, directly, no nonsense. He expects them to react the way he reacts, to do what they promise to do. He thinks relations between black and white would be fine if all whites treated blacks the way he does. If a man works hard, he respects him. If he does not, clear out. He'll take a hardworking black over a lazy white any day.

"We as whites say we're superior. But I say, if you're superior, you must show it, you must demonstrate it. For example, every child of mine must play a musical instrument because I think a civilized person must have some musical background. I want my children to compete with the best, not with rubbish. I want them to show that they are superior people. People say the bloody kaffir is this and that, I say that if you must stoop to criticize them like that, look to yourself."

The West, he says, doesn't understand who South African blacks are. Americans, he says, think they are all as articulate as Bishop Tutu and as committed as Nelson Mandela. The image that the West has of a politically sophisticated black population is the result of television. Every night in the West people see a small group of black activists in Soweto who *are* politically sophisticated. They are the ones who make news. Not the industrious black farmer in Bophuthatswana. All the Western news bureaus are concentrated in Johannesburg, and when they need some pictures or comments, they go to the same activists in Soweto. But Soweto, he suggests, is not South Africa, just as Harlem is not America. The blacks in Soweto are urban and Westernized and are as different from most blacks in South Africa as a Brahman is from a Guernsey.

Outsiders, de la Rey says, don't realize how many moderate blacks there are, blacks who are willing to participate in the political process on the white man's terms. Most rural blacks, de la Rey says, will be content with a sturdier roof over their heads and more food.

De la Rey, like many whites, talks about improving the economy as a solution to South Africa's problems. If the economy is increased exponentially, blacks can have a larger piece of the pie without having to decrease in absolute terms the white share. Black income can rise without white income falling. De la Rey says that no white man will sacrifice something he already has if he is not gaining anything by giving it up.

De la Rey leaves the farm without talking to Ben. When he does, the following day, Ben explains that he plowed a different field because he thought the one de la Rey wanted him to cut was too wet. De la Rey accepts his explanation and then asks Ben if he is taking in lodgers. Ben admits that he is. He reminds Ben of their agreement and boots him out of the house. He will keep him as foreman, though. He's a damn good foreman.

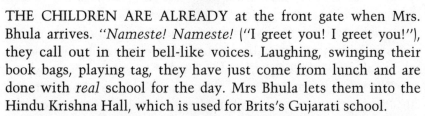

THE CHILDREN ARE ALREADY at the front gate when Mrs. Bhula arrives. *"Nameste! Nameste!* ("I greet you! I greet you!"), they call out in their bell-like voices. Laughing, swinging their book bags, playing tag, they have just come from lunch and are done with *real* school for the day. Mrs Bhula lets them into the Hindu Krishna Hall, which is used for Brits's Gujarati school.

Two afternoons a week, Hindu children in Brits attend Gujarati school while Muslim children receive religious instruction at the Madressa. Mrs. Bhula teaches beginning Gujarati, the home language of most of the town's Hindus.

After his father died, Jai encouraged his mother to get involved in community activities. Mrs. Bhula was fluent in Gujarati—she *thinks* in Gujarati, she says—and lamented the fact that young people in town could not speak or understand it. Why not teach it? Jai said.

Inside, the children sit on wobbly plastic chairs, two to a wooden desk. Three classes are clustered together in the same room: beginning, middle, and advanced. Mrs. Bhula stands at the blackboard, pointing to Gujarati characters with a ruler. The children chant the names after her. Their legs swing back and forth under their chairs in rhythm to the words.

"When the children get here," Mrs. Bhula says, "they have had enough studying for the day. It is very hard to get them to concentrate. After an hour, they beg us to let them go outside and play." She says this good-naturedly, but she feels that whatever she can teach them before they get too restless is important.

"Almost all the children know English best of all," Mrs. Bhula says. "English is their first language. Their second language is Afrikaans. And Gujarati is their third. It should be reversed, I think, with Gujarati their first language. But they speak English at home, and hear it on television and the radio."

"These little ones," she says, "are still learning the alphabet. It is difficult and takes them a long time. They also learn mathematics and the multiplication tables. They learn the tables up to twenty times twenty. Their fathers and grandfathers even memorized fractions like two and a half times sixteen. They could all multiply faster than a calculator. But these ones prefer to use a calculator. It is easier and less work."

She thinks the children of today lack discipline. "TV has done more harm than anything else. They are losing touch with reality. When I was growing up I used to go out into the yard and watch the ants and the insects. Now children don't play games anymore. They just watch television. If I didn't teach I wouldn't know. Sometimes I listen to them talk among themselves, and I hear them talking about 'Knight Rider' and 'Airwolf,' American TV shows."

Within half an hour, the children are fidgety. There are no curtains on the windows, and the hazy sunlight seems to activate them as if they were heliotropes. The girls, skinny and skittish, pull each other's ponytails. Mrs. Bhula calls them to the front of the room to inspect their notebooks. Five are gathered around her, their dark heads clustered together like a bunch of grapes.

The Gujarati school is a source of friction between Hindu and Muslim in Brits. While Hindus outnumber Muslims in South Africa as a whole, comprising more than two-thirds of the country's nearly one million Indians, they number fewer than a quarter of the Indians in Brits. The Hindu minority used to be dominant, but the balance has shifted. Muslim businesses have thrived and become the driving force in the economic life of Primindia.

The Hindus find the Muslims overbearing in their religious affairs and underhanded in their business dealings. The Muslims deem the Hindus lax in both religion and business, and a bit snooty. Muslim parents contend that the Hindu pupils gain an unfair academic advantage by learning mathematics at the Gujarati school. Hindu parents retort that the Madressa teaches the children to shun their Hindu schoolmates.

Jai does not like to acknowledge any discord between Hindu and Muslim. He knows that the Afrikaner relishes pointing out divisions within the black and Indian community, and he is loath to give them any ammunition. But he remembers how in grade school Hindu students often felt persecuted. "The relationship between Hindus and Muslims," he says, "was more acrimonious in those days. It was not uncommon for Hindus to be taunted by Muslims. Yet even by saying that, I am exaggerating it. In Brits, there is still an undercurrent of reservation about Hindus. Today, relationships between the two groups are cordial. But people stick to themselves."

Mrs. Bhula is less willing to gloss over the differences. She thinks things are worse today than they used to be. "The Muslims protect their interests," she says. "It only came out about fifteen years ago. In the old days, Hindu and Muslim lived like one big family. Now the Muslims dominate the town. They are the landlords and there has always been a shortage of houses. Soomar is a Muslim. He still owns the whole block of Kruis Street. We have rented our shop from him for many years. Sometimes, he asked for the rent three or four years in advance. If you complained about the shop, he would say, 'Go, I can always find another tenant.' "

As a parent, she finds Muslim families too conservative with their children. She remembers how she would give Gita permission to go on school trips, but the excursions would be cancelled because the Muslim mothers forbade their children from going. "I don't think they trust their children," she says.

After forty minutes, the children have wilted. A little boy drops a penny and leaps out of his chair to fetch it. He bumps his knee on the edge of his desk and starts to cry. Mrs. Bhula goes over to comfort him. The children interpret this as a signal that their lessons are ended.

"Please, ma'am, can we go?" says one of the girls. "Please, ma'am," the others chime in.

Mrs. Bhula's serious expression softens. This is all the encouragement they need. They jump up and scamper out of the classroom into the bright sunshine of late afternoon.

●

THE GRASS ON THE TOWN CRICKET FIELD is as trim as a putting green. The pitch is demarcated by a circle of painted logs, white hyphens on a green background. The metal grandstands are sparsely filled—mainly with the wives and children of the players. Morné, taller, younger, and skinnier than the rest of the players, is bowling. His club team needed him, and Morné would rather play cricket than study any day of the week.

The cricket pitch is part of the Brits Sports Centre, one of de la Rey's proudest achievements. When de la Rey first came to Brits,

he thought it was a disgrace that the town had no sporting facilities. Sports, he believes, are vital to the health of a town.

De la Rey had been a rugby Springbok, a member of the South
African national team. As a player, what he lacked in speed he
made up for in heart. "Rugby is a physical contact sport," he says.
"It's not—what would you say?—a very sophisticated sport. You
don't get attorneys and doctors playing it. In South Africa, rugby is
considered an upper-class sport, but it's not the upper class who
play it. They just watch it."

When he got to the Town Council, he decided to remedy the
lack of sporting facilities. "I went to the state minister of sports,
and I said to him, look, you created an area for Indians in Brits and
a border development area for blacks. You want people to come
from the cities, but there is no infrastructure here. One of the
things that attracts people is sport. He said, okay, he'll give me
R30,000. I told him that he must give it to me on the condition
that the Town Council will give two rand for every one that he
gives. I went to the Town Council and said the minister of sport
will give us R30,000 if we put up R60,000." De la Rey chuckles at
this.

Today, Brits is a mini-Olympic village: two rugby fields with
lights, a 25-meter pool, an indoor gymnasium, two squash courts,
eight tennis courts, two bowling greens, and a pistol-shooting
range. "I don't think any town our size in South Africa, or anywhere in the world for that matter, has such good sports facilities."

Blacks are not barred by law from using the facilities. "The
pool is open," he says. "Anyone can use it. But if I were a black
man, I wouldn't feel very comfortable using it. I don't think a black
or an Indian has ever been in it."

Morné's side is in white; their opponents, who are from a neighbor-
ing town, wear red. Morné's bowling style is unorthodox. He gal-
lops toward the batter, his arm rotating in a circle like a windmill,
then hurls the ball and half-collapses in the same herky-jerky mo-
tion.

He takes four wickets. When his side is at bat, an older fellow
with a beer belly scores forty-five runs. His teammates cheer him
on.

"Beauty! Beauty!"

"Good job! Good job!"

In the shade, behind the stands, some of the players are drinking beer and smoking cigarettes. The atmosphere is lazy, country-clubbish.

Morné likes the order and precision of cricket. The different functions of each player remind him of pieces in a game of chess. Morné's school team won their league championship this year for the first time ever, but they lost in the northern Transvaal semifinal.

"All the schools that win the big cricket competitions are Afrikaans schools," he says. "People have this idea that it is an English sport. It's not. The best schools," he says proudly, "are the Afrikaans schools."

Morné is friends with exactly the same number of English-speaking South Africans as blacks: zero. He, like most of his schoolmates—and most local blacks—thinks of English-speaking South Africans as foreigners.

"In primary school," he says, "we had an English medium [instruction] part. There was quite a battle. We didn't mix. We played rugby, Afrikaner-against-English. There were many fights. We called them 'Rooineks' [Rednecks], and they called us 'Rock Spiders.' We told them to go back to England. Afrikaans kids are, by far, more conservative than English kids. In things like smoking and drinking and girls, we are more conservative also.

"It doesn't really matter now, because the English, in some ways, are more accepted. I think it must be tough for English-speaking kids; they were in the minority. In a school of about thirteen hundred, there were only about a hundred to a hundred and fifty English kids."

By Brits standards, Morné's father is an Anglophile. "There is still bitterness among Afrikaners about the Anglo-Boer War," de la Rey says. "Twenty thousand women died in concentration camps. It cut down on our breeding stock. But things have changed tremendously in the last twenty years. In the forties and fifties, the English often spoke of England as home. We resented that. That too has changed. I have great respect for the British. I say we in South Africa are British in the way we live." He smiles when he says this. "Small plates on the table. Two forks, two knives. They wear suits; we wear suits. Our civil service is based on the British system. If you think about it, South Africa is very British, but people don't like to admit that.

"If an Englishman wants to stay here, he should be loyal to

South Africa—otherwise, he can bugger off. If the English think of England as home, then I am very much more for the black man than for the Englishman. But I would much rather associate with an Englishman in my house than a black."

Not long after he moved to Brits, de la Rey joined the Rapportryers, an organization of Afrikaner businessmen who meet once a month to discuss civic issues. They are a kind of training ground for the Broederbond, a powerful, secretive Afrikaner organization which is a virtual prerequisite for becoming part of the leadership elite. Every South African prime minister since 1948 has been a member.

"The word Rapportryer—I must explain what it means because it is important. In the Anglo-Boer War, there were thirty people who carried messages back and forth between commanders. They rode on horseback and 'rapportryer' is the word for the rider who carried these vital dispatches. The organization was founded to support business among Afrikaners. In those days, the 1950s, the English had all the business. We formed the organization to support each other. The Broederbond is much more political. Rapportryers is solely business. Today, the Broederbond wouldn't accept someone who hadn't been a Rapportryer."

Unlike many Afrikaners, he does not mind that English is one of the two official languages of South Africa. He even tells a joke about it. An American arrives at Jan Smuts airport in Johannesburg. Van der Merwe (the generic surname in all Afrikaner jokes), the customs official, asks him if he speaks any other languages besides English. The man says, 'Yes, I speak French, Spanish, and German.' Van der Merwe replies, 'Oh, so you're not bilingual?'

At the midpoint in the match, the two teams take a tea-break. A player Morné's age offers him a beer. Morné declines.

"Say, were you invited to the party tonight?" he asks.

Morné nods.

The party is an eighteenth birthday dance for a girl from school. There will be a disc jockey and pretty much everybody will be there. Morné suspects that his father will not be keen on him going, but he knows that his father won't stop him either.

"Are you going?" the fellow says.

"I think so," Morné replies.

●

LIFE WENT TO LETHLABILE YESTERDAY. He was sitting in the front yard of Solomon Khoza's house drinking a Castle when he stood up, touched his forehead, and said, "I must go to Lethlabile." He had just remembered: it was the day his cousin was to pay *lobola*, the bride price. Life does not so much make plans as suddenly recall things he has promised to do. His life always seems improvised.

He arranges to borrow a car and heads off. The road to Lethlabile has only recently been completed and runs north from town, passing through a checkerboard of fertile white farmland.

There is no sign at the entrance to the Township of the Future, but it is unmistakable. A dirt road leads into what appears to be a sprawling, well-kept town of shacks and small houses. The hundred-foot high-intensity lamps impart the feel of a clean, well-lighted refugee camp.

To the right of the entrance is the Beverly Hills of Lethlabile, large, modern houses with garages and manicured lawns. Some of the homes are quite grand, with elaborate tile roofs, turrets, and imposing walls. Most of the Oukasie community councillors live here. The only others who can afford these places are civil servants —teachers, nurses, clerks, and policemen (twenty-two live in Lethlabile)—who receive generous housing subsidies from the government.

More than half of the houses in Lethlabile are the original shanties provided to people when they moved. For R52, each person got a plot of three hundred square meters, a water tap, a toilet, and a Zozo house, which is a gleaming one-room tin shed. Each plot holder pays R3.40 a month for running water and garbage removal. Approximately two-thirds of the 3,200 stands in Lethlabile are now occupied. The current population of the Township of the Future is about 12,000. For a black man, Lethlabile was a mighty good deal.

Residents received an actual "Deed of Grant" so that they legally owned their plot. Until the 1986 amendments to the Black Community Development Act, the best a black man could do in

South Africa was to get a ninety-nine-year leasehold, and there were precious few of those. The contract also specified that the residents were to build a house on the plot within two years. Many have not done so, but the officials do not seem to care.

Hundreds of those in Lethlabile were tenants in Oukasie who rented rooms or shacks from people with plots. Although only people from Oukasie are eligible to move to Lethlabile, many of the residents here lived elsewhere, Maboloka, Ga-Rankuwa. They had merely to show some evidence of having been an Oukasie resident. The white civil servants were mainly concerned about getting people into Lethlabile, so they were less than fastidious about checking credentials. People from as far away as Soweto bribed local white officials to get stands. Today, Lethlabile seems populated with more people than could have ever fit in Oukasie.

Even the meanest little shanty in Lethlabile often has a vibrant garden. People take pride in their places. Everything is neat and tidy. One of the BAC's original arguments against Lethlabile was that it would someday be a vast shantytown. They no longer make that claim; that day is already past.

Life knows his way around the labyrinth of dirt roads. None of them yet have names. The people of Lethlabile are waiting for the local white officials to choose them. Life's mother's house is at the eastern edge of Lethlabile, adjacent to the "stadium," which is actually just a large fenced-in field where concerts and soccer games are held. A wire fence next to the stadium marks the Bophuthatswana border.

Mrs. Buys' home is a newish Zozo house with another shack built onto it. Her plot is bordered by flower beds: pansies, roses, and bougainvillea. Off to the side is a five-foot-high pyramid of mustard-colored bricks. With these bricks, she says, she will build her dream house.

Mrs. Buys is a cheerful, stocky woman, with pale, translucent skin. She works in the industrial area at Robert Bosch, a German auto parts manufacturer, where she operates a machine that forms threads on screws. She has been there for fourteen years and earns R4 per hour for a forty-three-hour week. Every morning, she catches a 6:00 A.M. bus, drinks a cup of tea at the canteen, and is at her station by 7:30.

She had been a member of the union, but quit last year. "I liked the union," she said, "but I don't like the people who are running it. The union brought the light to us, but now there are too many regulations, too many rules."

When Mrs. Buys makes up her mind, there is no changing it. One day she simply decided that she was going to move to Lethlabile. They were all living at the house in Oukasie. "She was the only one working at the time," Life says. "They discussed Lethlabile at work. She was influenced by her friends. She thought it would be wise for us to get compensation for our house and leave."

Mrs. Buys says that she had just had enough. "In 1984, I told Marshall, I can't stay here any longer. I looked at Mothuthlung, but I liked Lethlabile. I liked the way it felt. It was open and spread out. But mainly I couldn't take it in the Old Location. The noise. So crowded. People fighting with each other. It's much friendlier here in Lethlabile."

Life tried to talk her out of it. He was, after all, a leader of the resistance, and if he could not stop his own mother from moving, how was he going to stop the government? But Life was resigned; it was her decision.

During the first two years, the people of Lethlabile and Oukasie maintained a tense truce. If someone from Lethlabile visited Oukasie, he was heckled and sometimes stoned. If someone from Oukasie went to Lethlabile, he was simply ignored.

Now the tension is mostly gone. They are, after all, one large family living in two separate places. People visit each other with relative ease. Those who wanted to leave have left; those who wanted to stay have remained. But it is still dicier to visit Oukasie from Lethlabile than the other way around.

Mrs. Buys does not regret her decision. Lethlabile, she says, is a big improvement over Oukasie. "Everyone here in Lethlabile is always working. Even when I'm at the factory, I'm dreaming about how I can improve this place." She chooses not to regard her decision as political. In fact, she supports the activists who are resisting the removal. "I'm a coward. They're very brave. I'm proud of them. We must fight the government, not each other. They will show them what a black man is."

Inside, Life's uncle is using a knife to scoop out a piece of watermelon. Life's mother and aunt are sitting around the Formica table. Life's sister Sophie is doing the dishes. She is fair-skinned and willowy; Life says she has an "English" figure, which means tall and slim.

His aunt informs Life that the girl's family has rejected the *lobola*. This is the third time they have done so, and everyone is angry.

Lobola, Life says, is actually a Zulu word, but it has been accepted by the Tswanas. *Lobola* is the dividend paid to parents for their investment in their daughter. Nowadays *lobola* is paid in money. Formerly, it consisted of cattle and goods.

"The money varies greatly," Life says. "It depends on the quality of the merchandise you are getting," he says and laughs. "Usually it will cost you about R2,000, but sometimes as much as R10,000. Educated brides cost more than uneducated ones. About three years ago a fellow from Soweto married a girl who had Swazi royal blood and he paid sixty cows and two camels, which they imported from Arabia. Altogether, it cost him over R200,000."

The custom is for the uncle and aunt of the prospective groom to visit the girl's parents. The visitors offer a small gift called *pulamolomo*, which means, Life says, "be patient and talk." The price is then negotiated and when it is settled, the aunt and uncle leave to discuss the amount with the groom's parents. If all is agreed, the groom's family pays for the wedding, including the slaughtering of a cow. "The cow," Life says, "should be slaughtered in the yard, so that the blood flows there. It is giving something to the ancestors."

Life's aunt says that when she asked the girl's family why the answer was no, they would tell a story about a horse lost in the woods or a bird trying to find its home. No one could figure out the meaning of the allegory. Life says enough is enough; the girl must not want to marry. Much better that it is finally ended.

When his unrequited cousin appears in the doorway, Life takes him by the hand and they walk around the yard. The cousin is about thirty, and so thin he looks as though a stiff breeze would tip him over. Life does most of the talking, and he keeps hold of his cousin's hand the whole time. "I haven't sat together with him for a long time," Life says.

Afterward, Life bids everyone farewell. Nothing has been resolved, but everything has been discussed; that's the way it usually is. As he is leaving, his mother takes out a well-thumbed blueprint of the house she intends to build. It has been designed by an architect in Bophuthatswana, and she is very proud of the blueprint—almost as though it were the house itself. The plan outlines three bedrooms and one bath. The cost is R35,000, she says. Life shakes his head.

"That is too much," he says.

"We will see," she says.

Life's cousin Boettie lives around the corner. Boettie and Life played soccer together as children, and he became a fellow shop steward at Firestone and one of the original members of the BAC. When Boettie moved to Lethlabile, he was regarded as a great traitor, but he and Life have now patched things up.

Life drives around the corner to Boettie's house, which is one of the two hundred original government-built houses. The postage-stamp front lawn is bordered with yellow flowers which match the house's yellow shutters.

When Life spies Boettie on the front lawn, he lets out a whoop and pats him on the belly. Boettie has a sunny disposition and always seems to be smiling. Life saunters into the house and props his feet up on the coffee table. Boettie is a scheduling clerk at Firestone and also plays the electric guitar in a local band called the Mercy Brothers that specializes in American soul music.

Boettie has a German TV and a Japanese VCR. In the VCR is an American Vietnam movie called *The Last Hunter*. On the coffee table are some coasters from Sun City, where Boettie loves to gamble. Life whistles softly at Boettie's possessions, and Boettie laughs nervously. On the wall is a framed poster of three kittens with the legend GOD MADE US ALL ALIKE BUT DIFFERENT. It could be the national motto. Out of one, many.

Boettie is a leader of Lethlabile and sees a bright future for the community. "We'll have factories here," he says. "We already have many shops. One day, we won't even have to go into town anymore. And there is much less drinking." Boettie is a teetotaler.

He is less sanguine about Oukasie. "One of these days, the Old Location will be demolished. That is the main thing; the white man does not want to be near the black man. I don't care what they say in Zimbabwe or America, or anywhere around the world, the Boer can do what he wants to the black man here." Don't fight what you can't change, is his attitude. He sees the government as something akin to a force of nature; one must learn to live with it and just hope that its actions will not be too malign.

After a few minutes, Boettie tells Life that he is late for a rehearsal of his band. They are performing in a few days at Lethla-bile Stadium.

"Life, you must come," he says.

JAI AND HIS UNCLE TAKE TURNS locking up for the evening. By six, most of the shops on Kruis Street are shuttered. The stores in the CBD are closed by five. Black workers from the industrial area are crossing the railway line on their way back to Oukasie. They all seem to be carrying plastic bags of meat and vegetables. Without refrigerators, food must be bought every day.

It is his uncle's turn to close up tonight. Mabel and Henry have slipped away silently. Jai is glad to leave a little early; he wants to take a swim at the municipal pool before it closes at six o'clock.

Jai stops by his house before heading over to the pool. Two black teams are playing soccer on the field in front of his house. The field, which was once part of Primindia, is now technically a white area. The town is allowing black teams to play there because they do not want any games to take place in Oukasie. Under the State of Emergency, sporting events in black areas are generally monitored by the police. The police recently knocked down the goalposts on the field in Oukasie so that no games could be played there.

Ever since the Primindia pool opened earlier this year, Jai has been going there three or four times a week after work. The Town Council built the pool and two tennis courts just behind it at a cost of about R300,000. The Indian Management Committee had long resented the fact that they had no sports facilities. It was considered a great deprivation, not so much because of all the aspiring athletes in Primindia, but because it was deemed an embarrassment to the Indian community. Only poor communities had no sports facilities.

Jai views the role of sports in South Africa as a pernicious one. The state, he says, is adroit at using sports as a political tool. The government has recently allowed blacks to compete with whites on national teams. They have done this, he says, as a public relations maneuver to persuade the West that South Africa is changing. Afrikaners often assert that sports was where integration began in America.

"Sports is an obsession in this country," Jai says. "The Afrikaner attaches enormous importance to it. He sees himself as the chosen race. Whenever they're defeated by a person of color, it has a dampening effect on their morale. The World Boxing Association has links with South Africa. That's why so many South African boxers were ranked. A few years ago, whenever some poor white South African boxer was fighting for a title, there was euphoria here."

White versus black boxing matches are symbolic combats. Whites cheer on the white South African fighter when he is taking on a foreign black fighter. "But, you know," Jai says, "when a black boxer from abroad comes here to fight a white South African, the blacks will root for the black."

The state's approach to sports, Jai suggests, mirrors their larger agenda. "In the 1970s, they had great 'multinational' sporting events. *Multinational*," Jai says with emphasis, "not 'multiracial.' There were black teams, white teams, Coloured teams, Indian teams. No integration. Each team represented a different 'nation.' Whites proclaimed to the world that we had an open society."

Inside a cramped booth at the entrance to the pool sits a woman who checks everyone who enters. Only Indians who live in Brits are permitted to use the pool. To the right of the booth is a neatly handlettered sign that reads RIGHT OF ADMISSION RESERVED BY ORDER OF THE COUNCIL.

The woman in the booth is Coloured, not Indian, and is married to the secretary of the Indian Management Committee. Before working at the pool, she used to run the Primindia nursery school.

There are two Malay families who live in Primindia. According to the Population Registration Act of 1950, the government classifies Malay as Coloured. Several weeks ago, two Malay children came to swim after school. The woman in the booth refused to allow them inside, claiming that they were not permitted to use the pool because they were Coloured, not Indian, and the pool was for Indians only. No one in Primindia has protested.

. . .

The pool is half Olympic size, set amid a lawn of well-mowed grass. But the effect is spoiled by the barbed-wire fence that surrounds the pool. The place is nearly empty—only two mothers chatting along the side and their two children cavorting in the water. Jai can't understand why there aren't more people using the pool.

Jai does not so much dive into the water as flop. His body is shaped like a horseshoe when he hits the water. He has been trying to teach himself to swim, and he manages an awkward crawl. He enjoys himself. A pool is a luxury, whether or not he can swim.

Jai says that his father would have been very proud of the community pool and would have considered it a credit to Primindia. He was impressed by such things, Jai says. He always pointed out the pools in the backyards of the white houses in town. Money and material things, Jai says, were very important to him.

"It was difficult for him to show affection for us. But the house in a way was a demonstration of his love. When we were quite young, he was a bit tight. I suppose he wanted to teach us not to be loose with money. He had grown up poor, and I guess he wanted us to appreciate things." The emotional equation was that money spent equaled love expended.

His father's circumstances, he says, were the opposite of his own. "It was very, very hard for my parents and their generation. None of them had it easy. Their ambitions were mainly material. My father worked hard to achieve them, and I think he got what he wanted. He built a house for himself that he was proud to live in and he had a Mercedes-Benz. I think he achieved his life's goals." Jai says this more in sadness than scorn. Jai is so reluctant to criticize his father that he turns deficiencies into virtues, describing his father's aggressiveness as independence and interpreting his silence as approval.

In many ways, Jai sees his father as the antithesis of what he wants to be as a man—although he would never state it so baldly. Jai winces at the memory of the way his father treated people, both black and white. He sees his father as having been co-opted by the system. Like many Indians, he was both victim and victimizer, both an object of racial prejudice and a practitioner of it.

"I often heard my father use the word *kaffir*. I think he used it more when he was young, though. On occasion he was actually abusive toward blacks, which I found repugnant.

"I was going to describe my father as 'servile,' but that would be an exaggeration. I saw my father referring to whites with—how should I say it?—referring to them with awe and undue respect. Even as a boy, I thought to myself, they are coming here to buy your wares, there is no need to be servile to them. But he once said to me, you may have the education, but you don't have the experience. In other words, you have the knowledge but you don't have the wisdom. Perhaps he was right."

Jai wonders how his father would have reacted to his detention. He very much wants to believe that his father would have supported him. "I know he did not like my political activities. But he never ever said that what I was doing was wrong."

Jai sometimes thinks that his father must have known something that he didn't. "My father, I think, did not put me on a leash, yet somehow today I am a shopkeeper."

WHILE KEEPING HIS LEFT HAND on the wheel, Life fishes for something in his jacket pocket with his right. He knows he has the tape somewhere.

Sello and Moshe are in the backseat. They had been sitting around Matela's when Sello stood up and said they should take some food to Uniboy. Uniboy, along with a few others, had been arrested the day before for assault and was being held at the jail in town. All agreed, and piled into the car.

Life pulls from his pocket an unmarked cassette and shakes it victoriously in the air. He pops it into the car's cassette player and seconds later the speakers in the back echo with the cocky, angry, thrilling voice of Malcolm X.

"There is no such thing as a *nonviolent* revolution," Malcolm X says. "Have you ever heard of a successful revolution that wasn't violent?" Life laughs. "What is the only revolution," Malcolm X continues, "whose goal is to allow black people to sit next to white people on the toilet? *The Negro revolution!*" he cries. Sello and Moshe are slapping each other with laughter.

Malcolm X then laces into Martin Luther King, Jr., calling him an Uncle Tom, a prissy namby-pamby, a sellout to the white establishment. Life himself reveres Martin Luther King, but he is tickled by Malcolm X. He finds him intoxicating: so brazen, so angry, so contemptuous of whites. He seems to speak out loud the emotions that Life can barely admit to himself. Life particularly likes Malcolm X's analogy about coffee. When you say the coffee is black, Malcolm X notes, that means that it is strong and powerful, but when you want to weaken it, you put in milk, something white.

Life rejects Malcolm X as a model, but agrees with him in certain instances. "I think you cannot renounce violence completely," Life says. "How far would we get without the threat of violence?" Life believes that the government is promoting violence in the townships and instigating vigilantes to attack local leaders. "The Foreign Office is always telling people that blacks are killing blacks, and I do know examples of blacks necklacing other blacks. But the security office has a strategy that gets black to fight black. They use elements that are already there in the community. The UDF and Inkatha [the principal Zulu political organization] are killing each other, but I think the state is playing a role in it."

"We are a very peaceful community here in Oukasie. Many people do not even know there is a State of Emergency. And we are by all means prepared to negotiate. But all of our calls fall on deaf ears. That is what promotes violence."

Not everyone in the township supports the Action Committee. There is another rebellious faction which accuses the BAC of being timid. Some of them have accused Life of being too frightened of the authorities to be a leader.

Uniboy, says Sello, likes chicken and chips and they stop at Travolta's *kafee* to buy some. While Sello and Moshe order the food, Life walks over to Hyperdrank, the town's largest bottle store.

Bottle stores in Brits have a black and a white entrance. Blacks can use the white entrance and do, though no whites use the black. Life enters through the black entrance. The black side of the store usually sells cheaper liquors in smaller bottles; the white, more expensive in larger.

Hyperdrank is owned by Christo Bolt, the son of old man Bolt who started Bolt Bakery in town. Christo Bolt looks like a big-game hunter: deep tan, thinning blond hair, and a mustache that droops over his upper lip. He was a pilot in the air force and flies his own plane. He greets most of his white customers as though they had just stopped by his house for a drink. "I know most everybody in town," he says.

Sixty percent of his revenue, he says, comes from blacks. Beer is the largest selling alcoholic beverage in South Africa, comprising some 80 percent of the liquor market, and blacks buy most of it. Brandy is the second largest selling liquor and whites buy most of that. "Farmers like their brandy and Coke," Bolt says. Whiskeys are mainly purchased by whites; cane liquors by blacks. Mainstay is the most popular brand of cane, particularly in the flask size. "Don't even try to stock another brand," he says. His few English-speaking customers buy what he calls "class liquors," Amaretto and Grand Marnier.

Bolt makes special deals with shebeens and bootleggers. "The shebeens buy in huge quantities. We have special prices for them. They buy as much as fifteen hundred to two thousand cases a day. They buy it at R10 a case, and then resell it for R30 at night. They come in with trucks. I load it for them with a forklift. They want to get in and get out very quickly. I sometimes give them a receipt saying they are doing a delivery for me, to throw off the police in case they get caught."

Liquor licenses are granted by the regional Liquor Board. Usually, he says, they grant one license for every six hundred families. "But that changed about a year ago," he says, "Now it's like a *kafee*. If you can convince them that there's a need, they grant you a license. Even if there is already more than one per six hundred families, as there is in Brits. This town has two too many bottle stores."

After perusing the merchandise on the black side, Life walks over to the white side. "Here is not as bad as the A-Team bottle store," says Life. "Here you can walk over to the white side and they don't ask you questions." Life appreciates such small courtesies. The A-Team bottle store is named after the American television show featuring Mr. T, who is a great favorite among whites in South Africa. The Panorama bakery, near Elandsrand, sells Mr. T birthday cakes for R28. Life selects a bottle of Mainstay from the white side, and then takes it up to the counter on the black side to pay.

Sello and Moshe are back in the car, which reeks with greasy chicken and chips. Sello tells Life to hurry before the food gets cold.

The jail is just a couple of blocks away. When Life pulls up in front, Sello and Moshe practically leap out of the car and march inside. Life will wait. He doesn't like coming here under any circumstances.

Moments later, Sello and Moishe emerge still holding the chicken and looking discouraged. The officer on duty said that he could not accept food for Uniboy. Only prisoners can receive food, and since Uniboy had not technically been charged with anything, he was not officially a prisoner.

The jail is next to the local magistrate's court, and Sello thinks that some of those arrested with Uniboy may be having a hearing. They walk over to the courthouse, which is a simple tin-roofed building at the end of a dirt courtyard.

A policeman on duty outside the court gives the three of them a once-over. They know him and nod, and then walk inside and take seats at the back of the stifling courtroom. The windows are open, but the air is hot and still.

The district court sits at Brits and is part of the Department of Justice in Pretoria. The court may impose sentences of up to one year in prison.

According to Mr. Theron, the local magistrate, the most common crime is assault by one black man of another. "Nowadays, we try hard to settle it with a fine," he says. "The jails are overcrowded."

The magistrate is responsible for administering the laws passed by Parliament, the ordinances of the Administration Board, and the local bylaws of the municipality. Most of the old petty apartheid laws, Theron says, are still on the books, but no longer enforced. The curfew law, for example, which states that blacks are not allowed in town between the hours of 10 P.M. and 4 A.M., has never been rescinded, but it is not prosecuted. The magistrate is also responsible for issuing liquor licenses. Restaurants decide on their own whether or not they are "open."

The proceedings drag on, and Life wanders outside to have a smoke. He nods to the policeman, a stumpy fellow with a wispy mustache. They talk briefly in Afrikaans. It seems that he loves American cop shows and his fondest hope is to become a police officer in the United States. His all-time favorite program is the "Dukes of Hazzard," but he also likes the one with that bald detective—what is the name?—yes, *Mr. Kojak*. Policemen, he says, seem to get a lot of respect in America.

He has written to police departments in the American South and Southwest looking for a job. He thought they might like some-

one with his experience. So far, he has received a few replies, all
negative.

●

IN THE LATE AFTERNOON, the temperature drops ten or fifteen
degrees and a breeze drifts in from the Magaliesberg, sweeping
away the stale air, giving the day a second wind. The air has the
mingled scent of jacaranda blossoms, and charcoal being lit for the
evening *braai*. Often, at this time of day, clouds roll in swiftly and
a spasm of lightning will flash across the bushveld.

This evening, the sky is clear. Sunsets are a gaudy panorama of
pinks and oranges; the best show in town. By 5:30 the central
business district is nearly deserted. Offices generally close at four.
People abandon the town for the night; there is no reason to return
until the following morning. In the evening, Brits has the feel of a
ghost town. A few black workers, taking a shortcut through town,
move silently through the streets.

De la Rey drives down Murray Avenue, passing the black
women street-cleaners who are finishing up for the day. Brits, de la
Rey says, could easily afford a mechanical street sweeper that
would perform the same job cheaper and more efficiently, but such
an investment is regarded by the Town Council as counterproduc-
tive. These jobs, he says, provide employment for blacks who have
few skills and little education.

"People in the West say we whites can't survive without the
blacks. But we have been told by the government not to mechanize
so as not to have high unemployment. In the States, you can put
petrol in your car yourself. But in this country, the government
will not allow petrol companies to do that because it will put so
many blacks out of work. We have the technology to mechanize,
but if we mechanize then we wouldn't need black labor, would we?
And now, they say, we can't mechanize because that would upset
the human ecology."

The unions, he thinks, are doing just that. As soon as certain
jobs become unionized, he says, mechanization will be allowed. If
the street cleaners formed a union, the town would buy a mechanical street sweeper. Even in South Africa, where labor is cheap, it is

still more expensive than machines. If domestic workers unionize, he says, they will lose their jobs. Farmers, he says, can buy machines that harvest crops more cheaply than uneducated and untrained blacks.

"We built up South Africa in part to feed the black man. If we only had to work to support ourselves, I'm sure we could do without them."

On the right, de la Rey passes Bonro Motors. The place is owned and run by John Bonner, a gruff, heavyset fellow who has had an automobile showroom on this spot in Brits for twenty-five years. De la Rey has looked at cars here for as long as he's lived in Brits.

Three spanking new Opels sit in a row on the showroom floor. Until last year, Bonner sold General Motors cars and products, as he had for the past twenty-five years. But General Motors officially disinvested from South Africa last year, announcing that they were pulling out in part because of the U.S. Congress's Comprehensive Anti-Apartheid Act of 1986. In 1986, GM was one of forty-eight American companies—including IBM, Coca-Cola, Revlon, Warner Communications, and Exxon—which either sold or shut down their South African operations. For years, General Motors, which had the reputation for being a liberal employer, maintained that withdrawing from South Africa would only hurt the people that American liberals were supposedly trying to help. But GM withdrew without warning its workers, many of whom went on strike to protest. They were immediately sacked by management. GM sold their facilities to a South African consortium and also agreed to continue to supply $100 million worth of components a year from Germany and Japan, countries which have much less strict policies regarding South Africa.

Bonner doesn't seem worried about GM's pullout. The company, he says, will not let him down. "I worked for General Motors for twenty-five years," he says. "I was selling General Motors products. Now we're Delta. Some local managers bought out the company. It was a good price. But I'm sure GM still has a say in what goes on. We sell Opel cars, which is owned by General Motors. Business has been good. I can't complain. We have good products and people who still want to buy them."

He tells his customers that the cars are still being supplied by General Motors and that the GM reputation for quality and support still holds. Disinvestment, he says, hasn't affected Brits. He points out that Barclays bank is now owned by Anglo-American of South Africa. "The same people are running the same places," he says. In most cases, he notes, American companies sell out to the existing South African management, and then continue indirect investments in the company. Now, for example, GM South Africa is no longer prevented from selling cars to the military.

Most people, says de la Rey, don't understand the logic behind sanctions, and the logic is insidious. "The people most affected by sanctions," he says, "will always be the blacks. The real idea behind sanctions is that they will hurt the blacks so much that they will overthrow the government. But not one percent of the people realize that, either here or in America. The people in the States think sanctions will persuade the government to give the blacks more rights. But that won't happen with the strength of the right wing now. Sanctions will never achieve that. But if you want a revolution, that's a different story. Sanctions perhaps can do that," he says. De la Rey suggests that to supporters of sanctions, the end justifies the means—if it is necessary to harm the black man in order to save him, so be it.

The United States, he says, is only injuring itself in the long run. "If Mobil is to withdraw, the blacks will be put out of work. The people who gain are the Communists. A man without a job and without food will turn to the Communists. The U.S. knows, just as well as I know, that if the whole Western world abandons us, the Russians will move in. We've done everything to keep the goodwill of America. But if the Russians could get their foot in here, they would. That's my opinion. The U.S. knows that in the event of real trouble, that if they need South Africa as a base, they can have it. If we give way to the Russians, then we've lost everything we've ever fought for."

What they've always fought for, he says, is independence. "The development of South Africa was individual and independent. Initially when the Cape was discovered, the Dutch government didn't want the Dutch East India Company to settle the area. But they opened up a halfway station anyway. They chose to do it independently. That was in 1652.

"We started the Great Trek because of our independence. Then the Anglo-Boer War started because of our independence. Then in 1960, we became a Republic and left the Commonwealth, all because of independence. We were always threatened. They said no

trade between South Africa and the Commonwealth. That too was
a form of sanctions and each time, South Africa survived and prospered.

"Now, why this sudden change? That we must do what every
other country says because they will impose sanctions on us?
There are plenty of other countries who are prepared to step in. If
we wanted to turn our back on the West, we could."

Sanctions, de la Rey says, may have the unintended conse-
quences of strengthening the South African economy. De la Rey,
like many whites, points out that American companies have simply sold their South African operations to local managers at bar-
gain-basement prices. While an American-owned business in South
Africa is required to operate under the Sullivan Principles, the
newly owned and operated South African company is under no
such constraints. "It's like Coca-Cola," he says. "They withdrew
from the country, but Coke is just as big as ever. Do you see people
with fewer Cokes in their hands? Where do you think the Coke is
coming from?"

On his way home, de la Rey passes Wild Cats Video, one of the few
stores in town that is still open. More and more people in town
have videocassette recorders. VCRs were invented for places like
Brits.

The store is organized into sections: Comedies, Westerns, Love
Stories, and Thrillers. Of these categories, the largest stock of films
by far is Thrillers (one whole wall). Next is Westerns. Love Stories
has only a dozen or so titles and nothing that would get an R rating.

The owner of the shop says the most often rented movies this
season are *Raw Deal*, *Florida Streets*, and *Friday the 13th, Part 2*.
American movies are by far the most popular, he says. The favorite
actors are Charles Bronson, Sylvester Stallone, Clint Eastwood, and
Arnold Schwarzenegger. The number one star, without a doubt, he
says, is Chuck Norris.

De la Rey decides not to rent a movie. He does so only rarely
(Yelena and Morné like them), and anyway he has work to do tonight and a long day tomorrow.

●

"AH," LIFE SAYS, INHALING HIS CIGARETTE, "if I lived in New York, I think I would go to Hollywood every day."

Life's knowledge of America does not exist in time or space, but in a kind of supercondensed cartoon version in which Times Square and Beverly Hills are not on opposite sides of a continent but on the same street.

For white, black, and Indian in Brits, America is the place they always measure South Africa against. Each cares more about America's opinion of South Africa than that of any other nation. America is the audience for whom they all perform.

For them, America is still a beacon, the last best hope of mankind. In different ways, white, black, and Indian view the American experiment as a prototype for their own and each invents an America in its own image.

Life himself has a love-hate relationship with the United States. What he loves and what he hates can be broken down according to a formula: what America does at home is admirable; what America does abroad is sinister.

What Life knows of America, he knows via American popular culture. American soul music is the sound track of his mind. "Don't touch Barry White," he says animatedly. "He's one of my very best artists. Teddy Pendergrass. Stevie Wonder. He plays really good music. I even saw Ray Charles once at the Coliscum Theater here. It was before the sanctions. I can still appreciate Dolly Parton. But she is not one of my favorite artists."

Michael Jackson would also have a top spot on his hit parade if music were the only consideration. "Michael Jackson is very popular," Life says, "but he is playing tricks that the people don't like. His plastic surgery shows that he does not trust himself. That he was not proud of the way he was. I don't think it's necessary for me to go out and *perm* my hair because I'm black. I am what I am. This is the way God made me. It's a sin if you are trying to fight nature or God's wishes."

Michael Jackson, he says, is "trying for white." In South Africa, the expression has more than just a figurative meaning. Every

year, a certain number of people officially petition the government
to change their racial classifications. In 1986, for example, 387
blacks were officially reclassified as Coloured and 314 Coloured
were reclassified as white.

Life supports the United Nations cultural boycott which is
designed to bar entertainers from performing in South Africa and
prevent their work from entering the country. He says he will renounce any artist who violates the boycott. So far, that has not
been too much trouble for him as the UN blacklist includes Frank
Sinatra, Anthony Newley, and Shirley Bassey, each of whom has
performed at Sun City in Bophuthatswana. The boycott's organizers contend that by playing in Sun City the performers were
bolstering the Nationalist government's homelands policy and sup-
porting apartheid. The boycott also had the effect of proscribing
any foreign performer, however well-intentioned, from playing in
South Africa. Thus, the *Graceland* dilemma.

Paul Simon came to South Africa to record the music of the
townships, music he used to create a popular album that was antiapartheid in spirit. Even though his politics were "correct," he was
technically in violation of the boycott, making him the moral
though not the musical equivalent of Frank Sinatra.

"The Paul Simon record was a problem," Life says. "We've got
to cripple the entertainment business here. The South African minority spends much of its wealth on entertainment. We've got to
sacrifice some of our hobbies to deprive the whites of entertainment. It was a step in the wrong direction for Ray Phiri and Lady-
smith Black Mmbazo to perform with Paul Simon. They had their
reasons. But it was against the boycott. The blacks were being used
for the benefit of Paul Simon. It's like they've got to be led by a
Westerner or they can't make music. Why don't the Westerners
accept our kind of music the way it is? Why should a Westerner
put *decoration* on our own music," Life says. He cites the example
of white American musicians in the 1930s and 1940s who adapted
black jazz to white tastes. What is the difference, he asks, between
that and what Paul Simon did?

Life and his friends see American power as limitless and its ability
to affect world events as absolute. "America controls the world,"
he will routinely say. He views the United States as the principal
exploiter of the Third World and seems to think that if America

did not exist, the Third World would thrive. If America really
wanted to end apartheid, he sometimes says, America could.

Life, like most blacks in Brits, has an unreasonable belief in
the power of sanctions. "Sanctions," Life sometimes says, "are the
only instrument." He seems undeterred by the fact that the 1986
American sanctions bill has not affected life in Brits. Life believes
that whites will not be able to endure the deprivation caused by
comprehensive sanctions. "We are desperately poor already," he
says. "We are prepared to suffer. What more can sanctions do to
us? We eat only pap here. Americans feed pap to the birds."

At times, he will suggest that the American and South African
governments are actually in collusion. It is not in America's interest to end apartheid, he says. "The Americans want us to be
nonviolent. But that desire is in their own interest. But perhaps it
is not in our interest? Lethlabile is a project that the government is
using to get American support."

For Life, the focus of American evil is the CIA. Life and the
other activists are fixated on the CIA. They regard the agency as
omniscient so that not a sparrow falls in Oukasie without the CIA
knowing about it. He suspects any and every white person of poten-
tially working for the CIA. Whites are guilty until proven innocent.

"How do I know such a person is *not* working for the CIA?"
Life says. "He may be my friend, but it is never wise to trust a
white man. Ha! If this white man were my friend he would be a
very good CIA agent. Learning everything while posing as our
friend. Some say that it was the CIA that turned in Nelson Mandela."

●

JAI IS INTO BRUCE SPRINGSTEEN, the Talking Heads, and
Tracy Chapman. Gita prefers quieter music: Carly Simon and Cat
Stevens. But it's Broadway for Mrs. Bhula. *Fiddler on the Roof* is
her absolute favorite. "I went to see the play in Johannesburg," she
says, "but the theaters were not open then, and we could only see
a dress rehearsal. I loved it."

Jai craves Western culture, and the Western culture that he

knows is American. The only thing he does not like about it is that
he likes it too much. He wishes there was a South African culture
that could move him in the same way.

Jai feels a naive wonder for America. America to him is a
model of tolerance. He knows that the United States has its own
racial problems, but he believes that America has the will to do
something about them. America, he says, is a country with a conscience. The American Constitution guarantees equality; the
South African Constitution, he says, mandates inequality.

"In America, there is this sense of compunction in the national
psyche about what was done to the 'savages.' That guilt, I think,
now reinforces the human spirit. It seems as though America really
is a melting pot. And that there is some effort to help those who
were once injured."

Jai believes affirmative action is a noble idea (Afrikaners loathe
it) and supports what he regards as the philosophy behind it: that
blacks have been unequal for so long that simply saying they are
now equal is not enough. To him, affirmative action complements
the theories of Black Consciousness. Black Consciousness, the
movement led by Steve Biko, stressed that blacks must be psycho-
logically liberated before they can be politically emancipated.

American blacks, Jai believes, have a greater sense of pride in
themselves than South African blacks. A repressed minority struggling for its rights, he says, instills a deeper sense of self-respect
than a repressed majority doing the same thing.

"Many blacks here get so moved that a white man is concerned
enough to take an interest in him. They don't say that, of course.
When they bow and scrape in front of whites—I know that's a
strong term—it is the legacy of the colonial mentality. It cannot be
easily diminished. They might sound quite militant in private. But
they haven't let completely go of the old ways."

Jai rhapsodizes about the metaphor of the melting pot. He sees
America as a place where individuals can assimilate without losing
their identity, a place where people can remake themselves in their
own best image.

"In America, I don't think it's always 'us and them.' When a
cultural exhibition comes to America, people go to see it to learn
what another culture has done, and what it has to contribute to
their own. Here, the Afrikaner ignores such a thing. He feels he has

nothing to learn from other cultures. Afrikaner culture is rigid and insular."

At the same time, he resents the pervasive admiration of America in South Africa. He thinks most people respect America for the wrong reasons. "There is an emulation of America here. The U.S. is now what Britain once was. There's a fetish about American clothing, American products, among blacks, Indians, and whites. Whites may not like American politics toward South Africa, but they use America as a role model. To them, America represents the triumph of the little guy, which is how they see themselves." Jai says that Indians admire America because of its affluence, not its ideals.

Jai knows some Indians from Brits who have returned from visiting America and reported that all American blacks live in slums and are treated like second-class citizens. But Jai is undismayed. These Indians, Jai suggests, make their observations in a resigned way, as if to say, it is hopeless, blacks are mistreated everywhere.

Jai has heard of a few Indians who have emigrated to America and then returned to South Africa. They said they did not like the cold, or that there were too few Hindus or too many Muslims, or that it was hard to start a business. But mainly, Jai says, they confessed that they missed having servants. "You must be very wealthy in America, they say, to afford servants. Here it is easy to have them."

Well-to-do Indians have long asked the question: what good is money in South Africa if you are not free to enjoy it? The Indians who have returned from America have reversed the axiom: what good is freedom, they say, if you are too poor to enjoy it? "They have returned," Jai says, "because they would rather have servants than freedom."

●

A EUROPEAN PEOPLE FLEEING the Old World for religious freedom on a new continent. Pioneers in covered wagons carving out a homestead in the wilderness. God-fearing Christians encountering

dusky savages whom they fight and conquer. A young nation taking up arms in a war of independence against Great Britain.

In its large outlines, the historical mythology of de la Rey's
white tribe is a mirror image of that of most white Americans. The
Afrikaner regards the Great Trek and the settling of the American
West as parallel quests and sees the Anglo-Boer War and the American Revolution as kindred conflicts.

Each nation views itself as somehow *chosen,* as settlers of a
promised land. Afrikaners describe themselves in the same way
that Americans portray themselves: strong, independent, hardworking, and Christian. The Afrikaners see South Africa as the
America of Africa, a country rich in natural resources and endowed
with unlimited potential.

"The U.S.A. is one hell of a big place," de la Rey says. "There
are as many stud farmers in America as there are stud cattle here.
Yes, everything is bigger and better in America. Especially in
Texas, eh?" De la Rey identifies with American bravado. He relates
a story about the time he went to Colorado. He took a tour of a
certain cave and the guide informed the visitors that it was the
largest cave in the world. "I knew, of course, that it was not," he
says with a smile. "But so what?"

De la Rey, like many whites in Brits, is bewildered by what he
sees as America's indifference to the Afrikaner. "Why are the
Americans doing us down?" people often ask. They are constantly
surprised by American responses to South African actions. When
they see their government make some effort toward dismantling
apartheid, they are wounded that America criticizes them for not
doing enough rather than praises them for what they have done.

De la Rey believes America is sabotaging its own long-term
interests in order to satisfy the short-term necessities of its black
electorate. South Africa, he says, is the last refuge of democratic
capitalism in Africa. He believes that it should be far more important to America that South Africa not become a Soviet satellite
than whether or not it permits one man—one vote.

An axiom of virtually every white in Brits is the following:
"America has apartheid; it just doesn't have a name for it." De la
Rey maintains that segregation is just as real and pervasive in
America as in South Africa, only in the United States it is de facto
and in South Africa it is de jure.

Americans should look at themselves in the mirror, he says.
They have no right to feel righteous about South Africa. He has

seen American racism with his own eyes. "What about the South?" he says. "Not even just the South; I saw where blacks and whites live in New York. Why is it, for example, that the black infant mortality rate in the U.S. is so much higher than the white one?"

De la Rey cares about what Americans think of South Africa and he believes that Americans have a distorted and overly simplistic image of South Africa. "Many people abroad think South Africa is a place where people stand with guns. They have the idea that it is a country of war and violence. The stories that I heard about hunger in this country are ridiculous. We rank with those countries with the least starvation in the world. There is more hunger in Italy than here. What about the hunger problem in America—the richest country in the world? What about the homeless problem in America? I saw people living in boxes on the streets of Manhattan."

He, like most whites in Brits, sees a critical distinction between race relations in America and South Africa. "The blacks in the States are completely different than the blacks here. It's both genetic and environmental. Here, blacks are by far the majority. Because the U.S. has a white majority and a black minority, blacks in America were forced to develop. The black man in America developed because he had civilized people all around him.

"American blacks are superior to our blacks," he says. De la Rey would entertain an American black in his home long before he would ever do the same for a South African black. Morné's favorite television show—like that of white South Africa as a whole—is "The Bill Cosby Show." To many whites in Brits, the Huxtables are just a typical black American family.

America had it easy by comparison with South Africa, de la Rey says. Assimilating an oppressed minority is far simpler than accommodating a disenfranchised majority. De la Rey does not see any intrinsic merit in the argument that the majority of the people should hold the majority of power. As Morné says, "It's easy for Americans to say majority rules, because the majority is white."

The white man is superior in attainment, he suggests, but inferior in number, while the black man is superior in number, but inferior in attainment. Why should they rule? There is no reason that the majority, simply because it is the majority, is right or morally preferable. What South Africans fear is what they call "the tyranny of the majority," and what they want to protect, they say, is "minority rights." The connotations are precisely the reverse of what the terms mean in America.

"Wasn't it Abraham Lincoln," de la Rey notes, "who said that the majority of people always think the minority is right. We like that sentiment here in South Africa." Lincoln's point was that people are sympathetic to the minority view, since they know it is the nature of majorities to oppress minorities. In South Africa, Lincoln's adage loses its irony.

EVENING

THE MEETING WAS SUPPOSED to begin twenty minutes ago. Life and a few others are laughing and jostling each other in the dirt courtyard in front of the Catholic church. There is no hurry. There never is. Punctuality is the thief of time. Meetings begin, like everything else, when they happen.

Tonight a specific subject is under discussion. The Brits Action Committee will hear about prospects for creating a workers' co-operative in the industrial area. Alan Morris from TRAC and Taffy Adler, a labor activist, have come up from Johannesburg. Alan is used to the delay, and complains good-naturedly that if he can get to Oukasie on time from Johannesburg, why can't the guys make it from a hundred yards away?

The meeting is held in the rectory next to the church. Three simple, scuffed wooden tables occupy most of the space in the long, narrow room. Two exposed light bulbs hang from the ceiling. The curtains are drawn—or at least the curtains on the two windows that have them. The light is like that of a Dutch interior. The men all sit around the table and the few women take chairs as far from the center as possible, as though this were a classroom and they wanted to make sure the teacher did not call on them.

There are enough people for a quorum. Taffy Adler looks at his watch. Somehow, the very act of taking charge is considered too peremptory. A popular word and concept at the moment in Oukasie is "dictator." People rail against dictators in the community. A dictator is anyone who is undemocratic and who seeks control or "status," another favorite word. Life has been accused by a rival faction in the township of being a dictator, but that does not worry him.

"Should we begin?" says Life, who is leaning back in his chair, blowing smoke in the air.

"Where are Moshe and Abel?" someone asks.

"Abel is unable," says Life, and laughs at his poem.

Taffy suggests holding the meeting on Monday instead. This provokes general laughter. Monday is hangover day; no meetings on Monday.

Life leans forward, clears his throat, and says, "We are here to discuss making a cooperative out of the Alfa factory." Alfa Romeo left South Africa two years ago and their factory is still empty. Life nods to Taffy, and Taffy begins his presentation. He speaks rapidly, explaining what a cooperative is, the difference between owning shares and having control, and the voting rights of shareholders. It is pretty arcane, and he quickly loses his audience.

Whites alter the chemistry of meetings in Oukasie. The black participants are often reluctant to talk with whites present; not because they do not want to divulge secrets, but because they are self-conscious about their lack of fluency and education. Meetings that include whites will end with some kind of decision, but then afterwards the black participants will meet informally to find out how everyone really feels.

Taffy raises the idea of starting a car manufacturing cooperative at the Afla factory. He says it would be the first major workers' cooperative in South Africa and they would need to raise something like R6–7 million. Life smiles at this; they are about as likely to raise that sum of money as he is to be elected president of South Africa.

There are two types of meetings in Oukasie. Small meetings with specific purposes, and large, general meetings that are like township pep rallies. Life prefers the smaller ones. Large meetings are generally held on Sunday mornings in church and are high-spirited affairs, with music and singing, more like a variety show than a political rally. Under the state of emergency, all political meetings in townships can be stopped by the police so general meetings are usually held under the guise of being religious gatherings.

This past Sunday, Life spoke at one such meeting. By 10 A.M. last Sunday, the Dutch Reformed Church was brimming over with people. In the front rows, women in their Sunday best were ostentatiously fanning themselves with colorful handkerchiefs. Old men occupied most of the rows at the back, sitting silent and unmoving in pin-striped jackets that might have been pinched from a scarecrow. The windows at the side of the church were open, and dozens of children and teenagers were jostling each other for space on the ledge.

The service was led by Reverend Moatse, who acted as a master of ceremonies, introducing each speaker, as well as the local choirs or singing groups that punctuated each speech.

After one musical interlude, Levy Mamobola walked out onstage. Levy, a shop steward at Robert Bosch who is regarded as one of the wise men of Oukasie, wore his new powder-blue New Balance track suit.

"Comrades," he said, "we are facing a forced removal. This is no time to rest. This is not a fight we can lose, comrades. This is a fight we must win. We cannot rest."

"AMANDLA!" he yelled, and the crowd immediately chanted in answer, "AWETHU!" *Amandla* means "power," and *awethu*, "the power is ours."

Levy's voice is low and musical. He mixes humor and exhortation, and knows how to grab an audience by its lapels. "Comrades, the community of Brits is a proletarian community. We are workers. The unions are part of your struggle. Your struggle is our struggle. You are with us. We are with you. We can stop Brits any time we want. The problem of Oukasie is the problem of every worker in South Africa."

"AMANDLA!"

"AWETHU!"

People were having a grand time. An old lady in the front stamped her feet to Levy's words.

"But it is up to all of us to come together. We must be united. We must come together to force the government to upgrade this area. Comrades, we must not forget the past. In order to plan for the future, we must look at what happened in the past. Don't forget: people have been hurt here, people have been detained, people have been killed by bombs. More will die. If you can't remember the past, I'm sorry, you'll all go to Lethlabile!"

"AMANDLA!"

"AWETHU!"

When Levy finished and things simmered down, a group of schoolchildren tiptoed out. They sang a cappella, and performed a doo-wop step in time to their clear sopranos.

Life was one of the last to speak. He walked slowly to the stage, his shirttail floating behind him like a pennant. He spoke softly. People had to crane forward to make out his words. He stuttered slightly; his sentences began haltingly and then picked up steam.

Life said that the community must stay together, that they

cannot trust the white man. "We have a highly sophisticated enemy," he said. "He is prepared to use us as his tool. We can only overcome our enemy if we fight our disunity. The white man wants to make us oppressors of ourselves. We must help ourselves instead." He asserted that they must unite the township, mend their differences or else they would only defeat themselves. He spoke for only a few moments before his words fizzled out altogether. Only a smattering of applause greeted him when he finished.

"I don't like speaking in public," Life says later. "I hate it, in fact. Look, I'm not a good speaker. I'm worse than P. W. [Botha]." This idea tickles him and he shakes his head and laughs. "My other problem with public speaking is that I don't have it in mind that I should be a prominent person. I'm just one human being. I don't like canvassing for votes. Why should we go and canvass if the people think we are the authentic leaders? Why should I go around criticizing the opposition if you're already sure what you're doing is right?"

A handful of white reporters from Johannesburg newspapers had driven up for the rally. Oukasie is news, not big news, but it is a symbol of the government's predicament over forced removals. Life has been interviewed many times and knows that a few images on television are more helpful than long newspaper or magazine stories.

Life has no qualms about manipulating the press to his own ends. The idea of journalistic objectivity is not something that matters to him; the press is objective if it is on his side.

Life would like to control the way the press views Oukasie. "There are things that happen here that we want to keep in the township," he says. "You know, a reporter can come here and write that the black man is very lazy and that he sits around drinking all day. That women do all the work. That would be aiding those who support apartheid. That's what the white man wants to hear." Life is not ashamed of what goes on in the township—he just senses that outsiders would not understand.

"In general," he says, "the media clouds things over, rather than making them clearer. Journalists feel the press is quite liberal, but I think it is something journalists just like to think about themselves. You know, I agree with the former minister of law and order that the press is playing a bad role here. The press wishes to see action. So," he says with a smile, "we must give them some action to write about."

At the moment, then, there is little in Oukasie to write about. A sullen peace prevails.

No one has any questions for Taffy when he finishes. People have to rush to get the last bus. It is dark when Life walks outside. The moonlight is bright enough to read a newspaper by. In the moonlight the township looks less squalid. At night the sky somehow seems closer and less immense than during the day. Life lights a cigarette, and heads toward home.

JAI DECIDES TO TAKE THE MERCEDES to Pretoria. It's a forty-five-minute ride and the Mercedes is safer and more comfortable than the Volkswagen. The car is more prudent in another way: the Mercedes confirms that he is of a certain status and status offers a little extra protection.

Jai cruises over to pick up Navine. It is difficult to get Navine to come out these days. He has a small child and he works long hours at Vametco, the mining company just outside town. Navine is a chemical engineer and is the company's highest paid non-white employee. Navine has worked there for seven years, and is frustrated at not being able to move higher. The next step would be top management, and no Indian has ever risen to that level.

Navine tells Jai that he recently attended the Vametco Christmas party. Like most companies in Brits, Vametco gives three such parties: one for whites, one for non-whites, and one for children, where white and non-white are allowed to mix harmlessly.

After picking up Navine, Jai drives over to fetch Ahmed. Ahmed lives in Primindia's one apartment building; Jai just honks when he gets there. Ahmed pops out onto the balcony and yells that he will be right down. Ahmed almost cancelled. The girl whose family he was to visit called back to say that tonight was okay after all. Then her father called back fifteen minutes later to say that the young lady had changed her mind. Ahmed is not offended; he has yet to meet the woman.

For Jai and his friends, going out in Brits is not an option. There is literally no place for them to go. No bar where they can get a drink; no restaurant where they can sit down.

Pretoria is still new to them. Movie theaters and restaurants only became "open" last year. Under the Group Areas Act, people could not eat in a restaurant outside their own group area. Now, restaurants and cinemas in so-called free-trade areas can be open to all races. In 1986, seventy-eight cinemas were given permission to open their doors to non-whites.

They have not looked in the paper to see what movies are playing. None of them read any Pretoria newspapers—too conservative. Part of the adventure of going to Pretoria is the spontaneity of it.

Last year, when the laws regarding theaters were changing, Jai wanted to see *Gandhi* while it was playing in Pretoria. He called the theater to see whether or not it was "open." He explained that he would be with a group of people and that he did not want to get turned away. The manager told him, sorry, the theater was not "open."

"I don't know what came over me," Jai says. "I'd never done anything like this before. I said I was an American citizen, though black—I wondered whether my accent would give me away—and that I was appalled by the behavior of the theater. Surely the distributor of such a movie would not want it shown unless the theater was open. The manager got very nervous and apologetic and said that it was not up to him but to the Pretoria City Council. I said that when I got back to America, I was going to kick up a fuss about it. He became very ingratiating and said that he was sure that he could make special arrangements for me and my friends to see the movie. I told him that I did not want any 'special arrangements.'"

The first theater complex they drive by is showing *Harry and the Hendersons* and *Dirty Dancing*. A nearby theater features a Rambo movie. A third theater has five films; one is *The Untouchables*, which they all want to see. Jai tells the others to go ahead and buy the tickets while he parks.

Once they leave the cocoon of the car, the joking and bantering

subside. Their faces assume a stony expression; they are determined to seem blasé, unimpressed. This cinema complex was the
last in Pretoria to become open, and they are on their guard. They
walk hesitantly into the theater as if they are crashing a fancy
party. They are the only non-whites inside and they slouch low in
their seats.

After the movie, they stand on the corner and discuss where to eat.
No one has any suggestions except La Gondola, where they've all
been before. They go there every time they are in Pretoria. They
know it is safe.

La Gondola is a pleasant place that looks more like a New Age
health food restaurant than a trattoria. They order pizza and Castles. At dinner they talk about the camping trip they are planning.
Some of the trails in Brits were recently opened to non-whites. The
idea that nature can be racially exclusive amuses him.

Jai is glad to take advantage of recent changes in South Africa,
but he is cynical about why they have occurred. He maintains that
they have been made to persuade foreigners that South Africa is
reforming itself. Foreigners, he says, go to Johannesburg, Pretoria,
and Cape Town, where the fanciest places are "open." Then they
go home and say things are not so bad in South Africa. They don't
go to the homelands or the Free State or places like Brits.

"The change is cosmetic," Jai says. "And why, for example, are
movie theaters open and not libraries, like the one in Brits? Opening restaurants and theaters is something the government can do
that is painless to them and looks good to the outside world.

"The Afrikaner is obsessed with getting credit in the eyes of
foreigners. The National party has become very sophisticated in
marketing themselves. They have not really changed. Yes, I think
there are people in the party who believe apartheid is wrong, but
only a few. The Nationalists always talk about not being understood out *there*, how foreign countries don't understand them.
What about being understood *here?*

"Apartheid is about suffering. It's not about sitting in a restaurant or going to a movie. The state knows that. The believers in
apartheid know that by allowing a few blacks to eat next to them
in restaurants, they are not tampering with the basic structure of
apartheid."

Unlike many other Indians, Jai is not particularly concerned
about the swing to the right. He finds little variation along the

political spectrum. "I don't see much difference between the Nationalists and the right wing. The Conservative party is more liberal today than the Nationalist party was in 1948. Even today, the Nationalists are talking about petty apartheid; grand apartheid is nonnegotiable.

"In Brits, the CP people may put signs in their restaurants that say FOR WHITES ONLY, but the Nats don't put up signs. Célèbre, for example, doesn't have a sign, but it is not 'open.' They're more subtle. Moreover, they know that not too many blacks can afford to eat where whites eat. As Archbishop Tutu said—and I'm not fond of quoting him—when Mike's Kitchen [an upmarket hamburger restaurant] became open, Tutu said that it was all well and good that Mike's Kitchen was open to blacks, but that most of the blacks can only afford to go into Mike's Kitchen *through* the kitchen."

MORNÉ IS GETTING READY for Olga's party. He has put aside his church suit in favor of a trendier outfit that he picked up in Pretoria. It has a short waiter's-style jacket and a cowboy string tie.

De la Rey would prefer if Morné studied this evening, but Morné explained that everyone in his class would be there. He teases Morné that now he will certainly not get four A's. Morné confidently predicts that he will.

A rugby game is on the TV, with the sound turned off. De la Rey sits in his study looking over some bills and tomorrow's schedule. He will be traveling to a farm near Rustenburg, and he will have to leave at dawn.

De la Rey will drive Morné to the party, which is at Vametco. Olga's stepfather is manager of the company and he has agreed to have her eighteenth birthday party there.

De la Rey drives through the underpass beneath Verwoerd Avenue. Morné combs his hair in the rearview mirror. Standing at the edge of the spotlight made by one of the town's streetlamps is a black girl in high heels.

.   .   .

Every evening, in the shadows of the lamps on Railway Street, young girls wait for cars to stop.

Betty is eighteen and works in a shop in the CBD. She walks Railway Street three nights a week. Her family moved from Oukasie to Lethlabile last year and her father is unemployed. She is very dark-skinned and has closely cropped hair. She never lacks for customers.

"Married men," she says. "Boers."

When she gets in the car, she usually directs the man to drive down Carel Street to an empty area at the end of extension 26 in the Indian area. There is some wooded land and it is dark and empty. She charges R20 for sexual intercourse. She refuses to have oral sex and few men request it. She has an IUD, but many of the girls, she says, don't use any birth control. She herself has one child and is not married.

Police cars drive by but never stop. Afterward, the men drop her off at the original spot, and at 9:30, she catches the last bus back to Lethlabile. Sometimes she sees her customers in town at the shop where she works. She is certain they don't recognize her.

The road to Vametco begins at the very top of Elandsrand. The houses cling to the craggy, sloping terrain and the people who live here, de la Rey says, are the new Afrikaners: smooth, well-educated, ambitious.

Most of those who bought houses in Elandsrand assumed that the location was going to be moved. The houses built on the north side of the koppie are less than a hundred yards from the township. A narrow no-man's-land of bushveld separates the two communities. De la Rey does not believe that there was a cause and effect between the building of Elandsrand and the removal of Oukasie.

"I honestly don't think that the reason the town wants to move Oukasie is because it's so close to Elandsrand. If that was the reason, Brits would have developed in another direction."

De la Rey thinks Brits *should* have developed in a different direction. He says the Town Council had been determined to move Oukasie before Elandsrand was built, but once Elandsrand took shape, the removal became inevitable.

De la Rey understands the blacks' reluctance to leave. "If any chap tells you that everyone in the Old Location who doesn't want to move is refusing because of politics, that's bloody nonsense. Some of them don't want to move for political reasons. But there are a lot of them who are sentimental about Old Oukasie. One group says they don't want to move because it's where they have always lived. I can see merit in that. I wouldn't want to move either. If there's only one family who has sentiment to stay there, then there is one family then.

"But most don't want to move because of money; they just can't afford to pay for it. And I understand that, too. But I also say that most of them who can't pay don't want to work. For every side, there are a few stories. There's never just one story."

What has happened in Oukasie, he says, is that the best people have left. The families with employed fathers, he says, saw their chance and moved to Lethlabile. Those who remain are often too poor, too old, or too powerless to move.

A narrow dirt road leads away from Elandsrand across the bushveld to Vametco. At some point—there is no sign—de la Rey's car passes from South Africa into Bophuthatswana, where Vametco is located.

Vametco mines Vanadium, a mineral used primarily as an alloying agent for steel and employed in the making of tools and pipelines. Union Carbide sold the company in 1985 to a group of local South African executives but still retains economic links with it. The company was not affected by the U.S.'s limited sanctions bill as vanadium was specifically excluded from the bill by Congress because South Africa is the world's largest supplier.

At the guardhouse, a young black security officer stops the car and hands de la Rey a clipboard.

"Sign here, master," he says.

It is dark except for the flames shooting out of the top of one of the oil towers. Vanadium is mined in open cast mines, and there is a great gaping hole in the ground that looks like the foundation for the world's largest swimming pool.

The party is in a long rectangular building that is decorated with strings of Christmas lights left over from the summer holiday. When Morné opens the door to the party, he is bombarded with the insistent bass of heavy metal music. Candles resting inside brown paper bags filled with sand give the room a pretty, flickering light. No liquor is served, but some of the boys have flasks.

They are extremely good dancers and do something called the sakkie-sakkie, which looks like a cross between a square dance and the hustle. The sakkie-sakkie is done in rows, and the dancing is regimented. Morné gracefully leads a tall young woman around the perimeter of the floor.

Two of the boys stand out. Maansie is wearing a long black jacket with a Union Jack pinned to the back. His friend Johannes has an earring in his left ear and red nail polish on his right pinkie. Despite their alien attire, they seem to get on with everyone.

Johannes paints and sculpts. He views himself as an Artist with a capital A and a political liberal. "I get all my inspiration from the black man," he says. "I think black art is beautiful. The blacks are way ahead of us when it comes to artistic things. Did you know that before the first man arrived in the Cape, the blacks were already making murals and performing elaborate dances?

"Blacks don't want to be Westernized," he says. "Western civilization is corrupt. How can you expect someone with such a great cultural heritage to accept our corrupt ways? I don't think we as Westerners have all the answers."

Freedom in art is one thing, political freedom is another. "I'd be willing to give up exclusive restaurants," Johannes says. "I'd even be willing to share power with blacks in Parliament. But that does not mean majority rule. How can you give someone majority rule if they can't understand the situation? We must uplift the blacks first.

"No one in the West talks about the progress that has been made here. The things the government is doing. Raising someone out of their circumstances takes time. Time is all this country needs."

LIFE'S SISTER HAS KEPT DINNER waiting for him. She has prepared one of his favorite dishes: cows' feet. Three large hooves rest at the bottom of the pot. Life takes a knife, cuts off a sliver, and drops it into his mouth. Taps, Moolie's boyfriend, grasps an entire hoof and begins to suck the meat from it.

Life asks his sister whether his girlfriend has stopped by. Without looking up, Moolie says no. Life laughs.

"We had a bit of a skirmish yesterday," he says.

Moolie has an air of wistful placidness about her. She does not get involved in politics in any way, and doesn't pretend to know much about the situation. To her, the issue of the removal is one of practicality: Lethlabile is too far away.

Taps doesn't think Lethlabile is far enough. He would like to go much farther, to Portugal. Taps is a dreamer, Life says. He keeps a small treasury of magazines—including one precious copy of *National Geographic*—by his bed, and gazes longingly at pictures of exotic locales.

"You know, I would like to move to Portugal," Taps says. "Or perhaps Australia. But I really want to go to Portugal. I have some friends there. Maybe I'd never come back. The only problem is that I don't like garlic." The family regards Taps's talk of going to Portugal as if he were contemplating a trip to Mars.

After dinner, Life steps out into the yard. There is a slight chill in the air. The stars look so close that one could reach out and pluck them from the sky. Life sets out to find his girlfriend. Her family has a shop in Greenside.

"I can't go on like this with no money and no companion," he says and lights a cigarette. "My lady is pregnant. It's important now that I get married. My sister feels I must get married. She thinks she is doing too much for me. She says someone else must look after me. But my girlfriend doesn't want to use that to force me to marry her," he adds and smiles.

"I want a wife from a working-class family. I can't afford a lady who is used to the expensive life. You must always be buying things for a girl from a wealthy family. My lady is from a working-class family.

"Her family knows about me, and they don't like me. She stays with her second mother's family. Her mother was one of two wives —what do you call it?—polygamy, yes. Her father passed away some time ago.

"Even after I get married, I will stay with my sister. It's a big enough place. It's good to have some children crying in a house. It's hard for me. I've been unemployed for the past four years. I have three children right now. All with different mothers scattered around. One stays in Soshanguve. One is in Mabopane. One stays right here."

Life yearns for stability. The authorities claim that it is the radicals who remain in Oukasie, but actually they are true conservatives. They do not want change. They want security, permanence. They don't want to take a chance on a new place. They distrust loans and mortgages and someone else building their houses for them.

Disco music—the base notes reverberating in the night air—is coming from higher up in Greenside. Life remembers that there is a party and tramps off in that direction.

The house, a four-room shanty, is pulsating from the music. "This is not a house," Life says. "It is—what do you call those places that Eskimos live—*igloos*. This is a black igloo," he says with a laugh.

Inside, people are reeling. Liter bottles of Castle are every-where. Many young men have on T-shirts with political messages emblazoned on them. "UDF. LETHLABILE. ONS GAAN NIE DAAR NIE (WE ARE NOT GOING THERE). LET US FIGHT FOR OUR RIGHTS AND ASPIRATIONS YCW." Most of the men have drinking glasses, not wallets, wedged into their back pockets.

Life sits down on an old couch next to Jacob Moatse. Jacob is smoking Consulate cigarettes and Life takes one from the elegant green box. Jacob teaches history at a Catholic school in Bophuthat-swana. He and Life were two of the original members of the YCW, and were once arrested together in 1984 for a passbook violation.

Jacob finds teaching frustrating. "In history," he says, "I try not to use the schoolbooks. The Afrikaners' books are distorted. They teach Afrikaner nationalism. The books say the whites and the blacks came to the Cape at the same time. But we know that there were blacks in the area for four thousand years."

Jacob describes himself as a Marxist Christian. "In acting against the government we are adhering to Christian teaching. To show your fellow workers that they are being exploited is being a Christian, not going to church and praying for more manna from heaven. The Afrikaner prayed to God to help him kill blacks. That is what happened at the Battle of Blood River and that is the begin-ning of the Dutch Reformed Church in South Africa."

Life considers himself a Christian, and sees no contradiction in also practicing ancestor worship. Why exclude one? Betting on both doubles your chances of being right. "Christ was like a shop steward," Life says. "What did he do? He went to the apostles to tell them of the bad conditions in the community—just like a shop steward represents an ordinary worker who has been unfairly dis-missed."

Jacob has had quite a bit to drink, and decides to step outside.

Life goes with him. Standing outside are Moshe and Sello, both drinking Castle. The two men appear very glad to see Jacob and clap him on the back. The greeting is a little forced; they have an ulterior motive. Moshe asks Jacob whether he can borrow his car.

Jacob's car is famous in the township, a brown BMW with acrylic fur-covers on the seats and two large speakers perched in the rear window. On the bumper is a large I LOVE OUKASIE sticker. Jacob says all right, as long as he drives.

Moshe, Life, and Sello pile in. If there is a free ride, there is always a full crew. It's the same principle as a free meal; you always eat even if you're not hungry because you never know when you'll be eating again.

Moshe and Sello do not really trust Jacob. He is a little too flamboyant, a little too outspoken. While they were in detention for three months last year, Jacob was not picked up. Neither was Life. All the activists are extremely vigilant about "informers."

Anyone can be an informer. The police are adept at creating them and equally adroit at making someone appear to be one.

THEY NEVER QUITE RELAX DURING DINNER. They are always on their best behavior. Jai, Ahmed, and Navine are the only non-whites in the restaurant. They swivel their heads to see if people are looking at them. Nobody seems to care. A number of times, they lower their voices because they suspect they are talking too loudly.

When they get back in the car, the joking and kidding begin again. Despite the fact that they complain about Brits, at how dull and tedious it is, they seem relieved, almost happy to be returning. Brits is safe; its limits and rules are known to them. In Pretoria, they are like tourists who are not quite sure of the laws of the land.

Jai drives a little faster home than he did on the way. The Mercedes seems to float above the ground like a motor yacht. The roads are empty, and he could easily exceed the speed limit. But he never does.

. . .

Jai enjoyed the movie, but has had better pizza before. He finds evenings like this one both relaxing and slightly troubling. A night on the town comes with a chaser of guilt and causes him to examine his own convictions and motives.

"Often I wonder, am I involved because I'm deprived or because it's right? Am I political because I can afford to be? I live in a beautiful house. I eat well. I could afford to go to the sea for a few days after I was in detention.

"But you wonder about some people who are in favor of revolution because they are so deprived, not because it is right. Of course, it is easy for me to say that from my privileged position.

"Just look at Oukasie. Many people have a vested interest in staying and say it is political. For some, there are economic benefits by staying. I'm speaking of a small group, but it's always a small group. I question some of their motives. Not all, not even most of them. But some. For many blacks, it is easy to mouth off slogans, but hard to really examine the nature of things."

Very few Indians, he says, operate out of any motivation except self-interest. "Whites are so entrenched in the privileges of apartheid that they find it hard to relinquish those privileges. Affluent Indians are in the same position. They are secure and want to protect their security. They are in an ambivalent position. They find apartheid morally reprehensible, but they also benefit from it." Jai pauses. "I'm being very analytical here," he says.

"You know, when blacks say 'our Indian comrades,' I sometimes tell them that they should look at Indians as individuals, not as a group. Indians, like the blacks, are not indivisible. People can benefit from the struggle. If you own a shop, and there is a boycott of the white shops, then you are benefiting. There are Indians who are jumping on the antiapartheid bandwagon to save their own skins or who think it is good for business."

In the past, Jai has questioned even those who seem the most committed. "At university," he says, "I noticed a certain laxity among people in the struggle." But he cast those doubts aside in prison. "Yes, there is a factor of self-interest in the struggle, but there is an overwhelming humanity. In another place, a normal place, I would not be considered political. I would read the papers, yes. I would follow what was going on. But I would not be considered political. But this is not a normal place. One is political here just by being human.

"I can't pinpoint the time I realized this," he says, "because I don't feel like I ever changed. I can't find a moment of revelation. The passion for justice is like a golden thread running through your whole life."

Jai sees the sign for Brits. He has entered the town's gravitational field and grows quiet. His life is returning.

Jai drops off Navine and Ahmed. He pulls into his driveway and gets out to open the garage door. The Mercedes always sleeps inside. When he raises the garage door, he wakes up Shamu who stays with his mother in a room behind the garage.

"Ma . . . Ma," he calls out.

In the kitchen, Gita has left him a glass of chocolate milk, covered with wax paper. It's still cold.

Jai has been in the shop five years. The four-year period when he could still get his degree has passed.

"It's ironic that if it were not for politics I would have my degree and more freedom. I was very involved in politics my last term, campaigning against the House of Delegates, and I did not take my final two papers. It was during the next term that my father passed away, and if I had done those two papers I would have already had my degree.

"You know, I've been in the shop long enough now that I'm getting used to it. Sometimes I feel contaminated, inauthentic. I sometimes feel that my perspective has clouded over. That I am not the person I once was.

"I don't see myself as having any options. I've thought about expanding the business and finding someone else to run the shop. But that is not easy to do. I just don't see any way out."

BY TEN, THE PARTY IS OVER. Morné is talking with a small group of boys and girls when his father arrives. He says good night, and heads to the car. He's tired. Once inside, he slumps over in his seat and falls asleep.

It is late for de la Rey. He is not much for frivolity, but thinks the students should have their fun while they can. He looks at them, standing and chatting in the moonlight, and muses that he is not sure he would like to inherit their world. Things were simpler when he was growing up.

"Sometimes I think the future is ominous. But when I think with my head and not with my heart, I'm less worried. If only the external pressure does not push development too quickly." If only South Africa were left alone. That is one of the Afrikaner's unshakable beliefs.

"The whole international uproar about South Africa is based around the issue of what people call 'human rights.' But I think there is a great difference between human rights and political rights. I think the greatest human right is the ability to live; to be able to breathe, to eat, to have a roof over one's head. That's the utmost, the most important single principle of human rights. Political rights is just one component of human rights."

The Mercedes hurtles through the bushveld. The headlights are hardly necessary, so bright are the moon and stars.

"Today, when they speak of human rights they mean political rights. In the United Nations, when they say that the blacks have no human rights in South Africa, they mean political rights. When they speak about the people in Ethiopia or Mozambique, they don't say they have no human rights, they say they don't have any food. Why is that? What does it matter if they have political rights—which they do *not* have, by the way—if they don't have food? If it were a choice, what would you rather have, food or political rights?

"I ask you, how many people are starving in Mozambique? In Zambia? In Ethiopia? In Malawi? In Kenya? Now, how many people are starving here? They have their 'political rights' in those countries, but they have no food. Here, they have not fulfilled their political aspirations, but they are not starving. Which would you take? Surely the majority of Ethiopians who are starving would rather have food than political rights.

"In Zimbabwe, they are forced by law to vote and only sixteen percent of the people went to the polls. But how many people require food every day? One hundred percent. Political rights, I'm afraid, is a minority concern in Africa. The outside world seems to only care about their political rights, not about their stomachs.

"If there is majority rule here, the only advantage they'll ever get from that is political rights. They won't get greater economic advantages. I honestly don't think they'd be better off. The economic system would stay the same. They would still be disadvantaged. They will have political rights but they still won't have jobs. Political rights don't feed hungry people, and they don't make jobs for people without work."

De la Rey noses the car into the long driveway. The leaves of the palms lining the driveway softly brush the windows of the car.

"We whites," de la Rey continues, "have been convicted without being able to make our case. You know, I'm not convinced that the blacks are as unhappy as they're supposed to be. Around the world, whatever we do is too little too late. The only thing that is acceptable to the international community is to give the government to the blacks. If that's what it takes, you won't find a single white that will be willing to do so.

"School. Religion. Home. These are the areas that matter to people. If you tamper with a man's school, his church, or his home, he'll take out his rifle."

He pulls the car to a stop.

"If changes come too fast, the blacks will suffer a great deal. With more time, they'll have a better chance against us. But if the revolution must come, it should come quickly. We've got a chance now. We're militarily strong and financially strong. We should have the fight now, while we still can win it. Look at Rhodesia. At first they gave the rebels a hard time, but after fifteen years of boycotts, they couldn't fight anymore.

"If it came to it, I would take up arms to defend my country. I wouldn't think twice about it. It's a difficult situation. If we change too quickly, we'll lose our own people; if we change too slowly, the outsiders will kill us, not the blacks.

"I myself would never emigrate. No, I don't think the situation, even at the worst, could ever get so bad that I would leave."

MOSHE TELLS JACOB TO DRIVE to Primindia. He directs him to a house on Crocodile Street. Moshe gets out of the car, rings the bell, and then goes inside. Several minutes later he emerges carrying a large cardboard box. Life takes it and puts it in the trunk.

They then drive over to Carel Street and stop at an attractive modern home. Life gets out and rings the doorbell. He goes inside and then moments later emerges carrying an eight-by-ten manila envelope containing something the size of a paperback.

Jacob drives back to Oukasie. There is an air of expectation in the car. He is directed to a house in Vuka. From the outside, it appears dark and empty. Life gets out and knocks on a window, and a dim light flicks on inside. Life enters and then moments later comes out carrying an old black-and-white TV with a bug-eyed screen.

Next stop is Abel's house in Greenside. Cars and a truck are parked in front. Jacob pulls in. A radio is playing. Dogs bark in the night. They carry everything inside.

In the living room, Moshe removes a VCR from the cardboard box and places it on a small table. Life puts the TV next to it, and out of the envelope Sello takes a videocassette. Abel hands everyone a Castle. He has plenty, being one of Oukasie's leading bootleggers.

Moshe and Abel try to connect the cables. Each time they think they have it right, they turn on the TV and get a blank screen. Life wanders over, peers behind the machine, and points to something. They try that. It doesn't work.

It is hot and close in the room. There is much laughter, and no one seems annoyed or frustrated. It will take as long as it takes. It is all part of the evening. Who knows, this may prove to be the most enjoyable part?

Each takes his turn trying to fix the machine. Democracy, Life says with a smile. Many of the left-wing antiapartheid groups in South Africa say that it is not apartheid which is the problem, but capitalism, apartheid being only the natural outgrowth of a pernicious economic system. Life does not subscribe to this. Yes, he agrees with them that the South African economy is controlled by half a dozen corporations. But apartheid *is* the problem. What would be so terrible to have those same six companies if there was no apartheid?

"I'm not a socialist," Life says. "I'm a democrat." But he knows that dictators and despots always pay homage to "democracy." Everyone says they are for democracy.

Life is tired. They all are. There is a sense that the whole thing —the whole business of fighting the removal—has gone on too long. That any victory may not be worth the price of winning it.

"I sometimes wonder whether I made a mistake by becoming chairman," Life says. "I sometimes think things might have been different. As a leader, you have to take shit from both sides. I get letters from people threatening me. But if you try to mediate and lean one way, one side always looks at you as a collaborator.

"When we started the BAC we discussed whether we should affiliate it with any political group, and we decided not to. Our responsibility was to serve the community. We didn't want to have to decide about the political structures of South Africa. It would have been wrong to affiliate. We are all novices in the struggle, but we want to do things on our own.

"In a way, everything is quite normal around Oukasie. Some of the elderly people don't even know what's happening at all. They just continue to pay their rent like always. They do not know or care about the politics of the place.

"But you know we have always lived in a state of apprehensiveness. It's not good for us. We never know what the next hour will bring. The white man forces us to live in a certain way and then tells the world, 'look at the way they live.' But we don't want to live this way. We are living abnormal lives," Life says. He has another thought and smiles. "But that is normal for us."

Moshe makes the right connection and the VCR comes blinking into life. Moshe lets out a whoop. He is congratulated all around, and takes a deep bow.

Life grabs the envelope and opens it. Inside is an unmarked videocassette and he slips it into the machine. Everyone settles in. Moshe and Abel share the sofa. Life takes a wooden chair next to the TV. The others stretch out on the floor.

The screen is dark and blurry, and then suddenly the word MANDELA appears. People start clapping and yelling. Life stamps his feet. The movie is a bootleg tape of an American cable television movie made by HBO about the life of Nelson Mandela. It is technically illegal to show because Mandela is a "banned" person. Listening to the words of a banned person is a violation of the Internal Security Act. The tape has been passed around secretly, township to township, in a kind of underground railroad of banned images.

When the actor Danny Glover comes on screen as Mandela, everyone cheers. "He is so young," Abel says. But as the movie progresses—Glover meeting Winnie, Winnie weeping when she visits him in prison—the men find it corny. They don't recognize many things. Places and scenes are unfamiliar to them. For them, the film is not an exposure to the pain of apartheid, but a distraction from it.

As the movie nears its end, Life and the others grow quiet. Not because of anything on the screen—they lost interest long ago—but at a certain point, they all seemed to realize that when the movie was over they would have to return to the world that it was supposedly about. Dawn is only a few hours off. Life goes on.

AFTERWORD

IN AUGUST 1989, a Pretoria Supreme Court judge reversed the Administrator of the Transvaal's decision declaring Oukasie an emergency squatter's camp. In a suit brought by Geoff Budlender of the Legal Resources Center, the judge ruled that the people of Oukasie were not "homeless" as the Administrator argued, and therefore declaring Oukasie to be a squatter's camp was improper. Budlender argued that the government did not have a right to use a law designed to provide people with housing for the opposite purpose.

Business has been hectic for Dr. de la Rey. He is traveling more than ever, but his new fax machine helps him stay in contact with clients and suppliers. Morné is doing well at university and has been driving home on vacations—in his used car—to assist his father in the lab.

As de la Rey predicted, voting in the Brits municipal elections veered to the right. Brits Town Council seats were contested on a party basis for the first time and Conservative candidates won seven of the nine places.

Things at Jai's shop are little changed. He is thinking about trying to start a newspaper for the Brits area and has been gathering information about how to do it. He has stopped swimming at the Primindia municipal pool ever since the day, last September, when he took Shamu, and the woman at the gate barred the boy because he was black. Julia decided not to send Shamu home to Pietersburg, much to the delight of the Bhula family. Gita found a job as an instructor at a college in Bophuthatswana and has discovered that she loves teaching.

Early Sunday morning, May 21, 1989, Life was stabbed to death in a small field behind his house. He had spent the evening drinking and sometime after midnight, he and Moshe returned to Life's house for a final bottle of Castle. A short while later, a group of black men broke in and dragged Life and Moshe outside. Moshe was wounded, but survived. The killers were thought to be members of a rival faction in the township who accused Life and the BAC of being too conciliatory to the authorities. A number of men were arrested, but no one was charged with the crime.

Life's mother, the legal guardian of the body, arranged for her son to be buried at Lethlabile. The funeral took place at Lethlabile's main cemetery on a Monday morning at 7 A.M. The BAC wanted to hold the ceremony on a Saturday night, but under the state's emergency regulations, funerals like Life's cannot be held on weekends. Only a handful of people made it to the burial.

ACKNOWLEDGMENTS

My debt to the three families who are at the heart of this book is obvious. They opened their lives to me and never complained about the nuisance I made. In Brits, I want to thank Marguerite Myburgh for her abiding kindness and many others for their time and knowledge: Manus van Rensburg, Japie Steenkamp, Hein Enslin, Deon Erasmus, Charles and Nathan Lakier, John Cunnif, Levy Mamobolo, Sello Ramakopya, Moshe Mahlaela, Ismail Majam, and Wonder.

Alan Morris's role in the book was central: he introduced me to Brits, and his experience, insight, and courage guided me at nearly every turn. Geoff Budlender was always patient and clear in explaining things three and four times. Joan Lombard provided able help with local research. Many others in South Africa helped in ways large and small, and I am grateful to each of them.

Jann Wenner, Susan Murcko, and Bob Wallace of *Rolling Stone* first sent me to South Africa to write about it. The generosity of my editors at *Time*, Jason McManus, Henry Muller, Dick Duncan, and Walter Isaacson, made what was difficult seem easy. Lynn Hirschberg, David Michaelis, and Jim Kelly read the manuscript and gave astute counsel. Kate Monick kept the fires burning while I was away; Robert Gibbs provided unfailing support when I was home.

My editor, Alice Mayhew, understood implicitly what I was trying to do and gave me the confidence to do it. At Simon and Schuster, I am also obliged to George Hodgman for his tireless assistance. My agent, Tim Seldes, contributed sage advice each step of the way.